"This book comes like a tall glass of cold water on a hot day. For too long, we have been writing sermons, as if people were going to read them instead of listen to them. Dave McClellan believes that if our sermons are going to be heard, we need to speak them into being. He is right. This is an engaging book, entirely relevant to our present moment. I can't wait to hear the preaching that results."

Kenton C. Anderson, President and Dean, Northwest Baptist Seminary; Professor of Homiletics, ACTS Seminaries of Trinity Western University

"Sermons are delivered orally, so why should they be conceived and gestate in literacy? Using Augustine, Plato, Aristotle, and especially Quintilian, *Preaching by Ear* explores the art and science of orality. Homiletics owes much to classical rhetoric, and McClellan continues to show us why. He challenges us to live lives of curiosity and worship, study and pray ourselves deep into the text, 'map' (not outline) the sermon, practice aloud, and then step out in faith without the safety net (or is it a straightjacket?) of written notes. Written by a pastor and scholar, *Preaching by Ear* will inform and challenge you."

Jeffrey D. Arthurs, Professor of Preaching and Communication; Chair, Division of Practical Theology, Gordon-Conwell Theological Seminary

"If we preach sermons for listening congregations, why prepare them for readers? But since the printing press, sermons have moved from memorable oral patterns to the forgettable patterns of the written word. *Preaching by Ear* invites pastors to prepare messages for *auditoriums*—the communication environment of people in church—and to engage listeners through premeditated (not pre-scripted) preaching. This volume revitalizes content-rich, Scriptural preaching by pastors for listeners like us through the principles of oral thought."

Calvin L. Troup, Associate Professor; Director, Rhetoric PhD Program, Department of Communication and Rhetorical Studies, Duquesne University

"McClellan understands the embodied miracle of communication, in which speech reaches from the vocal chambers and mind of the speaker to the ear and interiority of the listener, heart speaking to heart. In the authenticity of his preaching life, he also knows the commitment of putting one's whole life at the service of the Word. In his scholarship, Pastor McClellan has paid forward his understanding of the arts of rhetoric and his love of the preaching life to hundreds of preachers—and I am one of them. Like Cicero and Augustine, and with the clarity of seasoned insight, McClellan knows how to teach, to delight, to persuade."

Gregory Heille, OP, Professor of Homiletics, Aquinas Institute of Theology;
Past President, Academy of Homiletics

PREACHING
by EAR

PREACHING
by EAR

Speaking God's Truth from the Inside Out

DAVE MCCLELLAN
with Karen McClellan

LEXHAM PRESS

Print ISBN 9781683592167
Digital ISBN 9781683592174

Cover: Dale Pease | walking-stick.com
Interior design and typesetting: John Bjorlie
Editing: Paul J. Brinkerhoff

To Karen,
the most present person I'll ever know.

CONTENTS

ACKNOWLEDGMENTS

I want to thank my wife, Karen, for co-laboring with me in all the wondrous and messy overlap of life and preaching and for her keen insight into both. My kids, Kelsey and Kyle, graciously sat through hundreds of sermons from a dad whose flaws they know firsthand. Kyle's philosophical insights and editing in chapter 4 were particularly helpful.

I'm grateful also for my longtime friend and mentor, Kevin Huggins, who has been a source of grace and truth over many years. As another longtime friend, Cliff Staton has walked with me through thick and thin, and spoken truth to me with such compelling tenderness. Chip Weisel's patient direction over many lunches kept me grappling with grace when I needed it the most. Knute Larson saw something in a young and brash youth pastor and graciously allowed me to grow in my preaching.

While at Denver Seminary, it was Haddon Robinson who first showed me the freedom of knowing just one simple thing to say. Dr. Calvin Troup and Dr. Richard Arnett of Duquesne University offered eye-opening insights into building a philosophy of communication flowing from the ancient world. Although I never had the chance to know Walter Ong, his winsome scholarship changed the course of my preaching and my life.

Finally, I'm deeply indebted to the congregation of The Chapel at Tinkers Creek in Streetsboro, Ohio, for blessing my efforts to learn to preach by ear, week in and week out, for more than ten years now.

PROLOGUE

We stand, as preachers, at the end of a long line of people before us. Like them, we have a word from God. Like them, we try to pass it along accurately. Like them, we look forward to or dread the upcoming Sunday. Like them, we have our bad weeks; and like them, we feel the amazing privilege and joy. Despite all our technology, the essential act of preaching remains unchanged through all these centuries. It's still a preacher, a book, a gathering of God's people.

If this thing we call preaching is as old as the hills, what new can be said about it? Not a lot. But perhaps that's the wrong question. Newer isn't always better. What if there were some good things our ancestors used to know and practice that have gradually and, almost imperceptibly, fallen out of vogue? What if technology, while helping us, has also eroded some crucial elements? What if we could step back in time and recover those things in a way that is helpful for us today? Let's consider this calling from historical, biblical, and practical standpoints. Let's try to get to the essence of what has, down through the ages, fueled a good sermon.

I've been preaching for a couple of decades now. It's been a journey. I had no idea how preaching would change me over the years. As a young preacher I was full of ambition and promise. Brimming with confidence, I was sure that God would use me in powerful ways. But preaching has a way of exposing our true selves. I've had to come face-to-face with why I even preach in the first place. I've had to look at my deeper motivations and the ways I sometimes use preaching to feed my own empty soul. I've seen how preaching is so much more than technique or study. It's the overflow of a life toward others. It really is—and I mean not just hypothetically—supposed to be more about people than me. It's my life that should drive my preaching, not preaching that should drive my life. Many of you have had similar discoveries. So we're in this together, you and I. And thousands of others this week.

Let's consider where we stand, as preachers, on a continuum. Some of us are comfortable preaching. That is, the act of standing before people and saying something is not particularly stressful. In fact, there is a natural enjoyment of that role, or what we have come to call a "giftedness." Words come freely; our style is fluent.

Then there's the other end of this continuum: those of us who feel the daunting challenge of getting the sermon out of our mouths. It's not like we don't have things we feel strongly about. But we stress over how the words will all tumble out. We fear "freezing up" or starting a sentence we don't know how to finish. We sometimes wonder if anybody really "gets" what we're saying, and we long to be more fluent.

Now most of us fall somewhere between these two extremes. You might think a book about oral preaching would be addressed to only those who struggle with fluency. But the kind of orality I'm advocating here has something for every preacher along the spectrum.

For those of us who struggle with fluency, this oral approach can provide some alternate ways to prepare and deliver that can significantly improve our ability to speak more freely. There are some ways to help unblock the route between the text and our tongues so that the things we want so badly to say can be clearly and passionately said.

To those of us comfortable on our feet, I want to talk about our need for deep connections to our text. We have enough fluency that it's not only easy but tempting to rely on our natural giftedness. We can make things sound intriguing. We can tell a good story. We can pass things along. But we might quickly evaluate a text on how well it will preach instead of sitting with it long enough to change us. In other words, we can end up talking about things that, while true, don't really move us. They sound good, but they're more on the surface than coming from someplace deep inside. They're not truly coming from the heart. To the extent this is true, we're hiding behind our fluency.

So those might be the two extremes. But as preachers we strive to be both verbally fluent and deeply grounded. Perhaps that's what we mean when we talk about "speaking from the heart." It seems to me, wherever we find ourselves in this mix, we need to be increasingly speaking from the heart.

That's the goal of this approach. To speak from the inside out. Our flocks need to hear God's Word coming from our mouths in a compelling, convincing way, with passion and conviction. There is a freedom that comes when our hearts and our tongues find a connection and we stumble onto something we can't help but speak authentically. It's happened to all of us at one time or another. Maybe for just a few sentences or maybe an entire sermon. We feel lifted out of our notes or our funny story into someplace different. We find the words coming from someplace deep inside. For a moment, everybody in the room can sense it.

Jesus talks about this when he gives instructions for what to do when he's gone. He anticipates the day when those who follow him are called upon to testify in front of the authorities. It's a highly stressful environment. He says quite simply that we are not to be anxious about what to say or how to say it. He says the right word will be given in the moment. He even says it won't be us, but the Spirit of our Father working in us (Luke 12:11–12).

While none of us would feel comfortable assigning everything we say to God's own mouth, there is a legitimate sense of words being given in a particular moment. But how would that actually happen? Does that mean we don't prepare? Or if we do prepare, how does it affect our preparation? Although we can't force this kind of "magic moment," how do we welcome God into our sermons both during preparation and delivery? These are the questions that we'll pursue together.

So where do we begin? Part 1 (chaps. 1–4) is about the preacher, because the preacher and the sermon are inextricably linked. For good or for bad, preachers are inseparable from their preaching. To try to work on preaching without addressing the person behind it, is like analyzing the health of a plant without considering the environment in which it grows.

To do this we'll consult both Scripture and the ancient world out of which Scripture flowed. We'll get a feel for a world where the preacher and the sermon were more naturally comingled. In the next chapter, St. Augustine will be our starting point, both for his own profound insights, and also for the way he points us toward classical Greco-Roman rhetoric. His seamless synthesis of Scripture, theology, and rhetoric brings all those worlds into focus. However, the reader who would rather start with inductive study of Scripture alone might be advised to start with chapter 5 for foundational grounding before jumping back to chapter 2.

In chapter 3 we'll move from Augustine to Aristotle and examine how this father of all theory and practice of public speaking coins the term *ethos* to describe something amazing that can happen between preacher and congregation as a sermon is unfolding.

In chapter 4 we'll proceed forward in time to the communicative context of the early church. Roman educator Quintilian will serve as our guide to demonstrate the absolutely crucial link between character and speaking. He was teaching public speaking in Rome during the formation of the early church. His thinking reflects the environment in which Jesus and the apostles preached.

In Part 2 (chaps. 5–9) we'll begin to draw an orally based model of preparation and delivery of sermons from some of these ancient thinkers and from the groundbreaking contemporary scholarship of Jesuit Walter Ong. Chapter 5 examines the nature of sound itself and why it matters to God. Sound has some theological ramifications for our understanding of revelation and how we were designed to assimilate God's Word. We'll examine how the Bible actually reflects this ancient oral orientation in the very way it is composed and how it talks about itself.

In chapter 6 we'll dig deeply into Jesuit scholar Walter Ong's expansive scholarship and see how the printing press literally and literarily changed the world. Since Gutenberg, we think differently about revelation, Scripture, and sermons. We'll look at many of the weaknesses of literacy and the numbing, depersonalizing effect it can have when it gets out of balance.

Chapter 7 builds a case for context in preaching, including preaching through entire Bible books. Gone is the need to "come up with" a sermon, replaced by the challenge of uncovering the sermon that's "already there." This will include knowing when to read, paraphrase, emphasize, and memorize the scriptural text.

Chapter 8 demonstrates how the sermon text becomes the devotional focus of the preacher's week, personally internalized and integrated into a variety of conversations. We'll see how an oral preacher actually functions in a typical week and how to build a road map to visually depict the sermon's flow.

Chapter 9 challenges preachers to embrace a more extemporaneous tone. By fostering a sense of discovery, ideas are verbalized in the moment to a specific audience and enjoy a flexibility impossible in a purely literary context.

PART 1

PREPARING THE PREACHER

1

SOMETHING OLD, SOMETHING NEW

Every age has its own outlook. It is specially good at seeing certain truths and specially liable to make certain mistakes. We all, therefore, need the books that will correct the characteristic mistakes of our own period. . . . The only palliative is to keep the clean sea breeze of the centuries blowing through our minds, and this can be done only by reading old books.

C. S. Lewis, "Introduction" to Athanasius, *On the Incarnation*

I was raised with the expectation and desire to be . . . what's the word? If we phrase it nicely it would be "influential" or "effective" or "excellent." A simpler word would be "great." I wanted to be a great preacher. Coming from a long line of preachers, I felt like I had a destiny that was waiting to be fulfilled.

The Pressure's On

As a thirty-something-year-old youth pastor, I was asked to preach in what we came to call "Big Church" (which meant the main service). It was prime time. With teens I had learned to speak informally. I would prepare, but I didn't really care how it came out. Speaking to junior highers, especially, taught me to be flexible and adapt on the fly. What's interesting to me now is that, in the pressure of preaching to adults, I abandoned everything I had learned about flexibility, and crafted what seemed like the safer alternative:

a manuscript sermon. I needed control over each phrase. There was no room for error. This was no youth group; this had to be good.

I wordsmithed the manuscript until I thought it was as close to perfect as I could get. Then I read it over and over until I had it virtually memorized. On Sunday I read it, but tried hard to disguise the fact that I was reading. I used my best acting skill to make it seem like all these words were just effortlessly spilling out of me. I don't even remember what I spoke on. But I can still picture that manuscript. My safety. My sure thing.

When I finished the sermon, I felt pretty good. In those days all sermons in Big Church were recorded on cassette tapes, so of course I secured a few. I sent one to a friend of mine from college days for "feedback." Actually, I was hoping more for kudos than feedback. But, oddly enough, I got feedback. My friend said that the sermon was pretty good. But that it didn't sound like me. I protested. Didn't sound like me? He said it sounded kind of stiff—like it was a preaching persona and not just Dave speaking. I remember feeling confused and provoked. I knew what he meant. It was a persona. Real Dave, the Dave that people knew outside the sermon, could never craft precise words like that in the moment. But that's what I was trying to present to people: something a little better than Real Dave.

I thought a lot about that. I didn't like what he said. But I was scared of giving up the safety of the script. So I resolved not to do that again. I resolved that if I was ever asked to preach again that I would take the risk of sounding more like myself. I would be willing to lose some of the polish to gain a sense of authenticity.

Risky Preaching

So let's talk about a style of preaching that is—well, a little risky. The oral orientation is a movement away from safety and predictability. It's a move toward vulnerability with a hint of the spontaneous. It's not knowing exactly where you'll go next. It has an openness, an unfinishedness. It pulls deeply from internal resources: emotion, experience, firsthand acquaintance with truth. It requires the preacher to speak into a live moment from a whole heart.

Think about political speeches. There was a time, not that long ago, when politicians could speak off the cuff. Some still attempt it. But it's risky. With every word they say being recorded, any gaffe will be replayed over and over. Most of the important speeches now use the teleprompter to hold the speaker to a very precise and prearranged plan. Some get pretty good at it. But if you watch their eyes carefully you'll see them going ever so slightly back and forth, working their way through the script. You don't really need to watch—just listen. People don't compose like that in ordinary conversation. There's too much polish. Spot-on metaphors flow out effortlessly. Sound bite follows sound bite. It's good language, good writing, but it's not natural. It's a persona.

Recently there's been a resurgence of interest in preaching without notes. There are books written specifically to teach that approach. But oral homiletics is different. Having or not having notes is not the point. We might memorize a manuscript and not have any notes when we preach. But that's not "preaching by ear." Preaching by ear is this: speaking from personally held, deep convictions in a way that enables our words to unfold in the moment by considering the actual people present with us. We are well-prepared, but we're not certain exactly how it will come out of our mouths.

Of course the counterfeit version of this is that of the thrill-seeker. For this preacher, the higher risk brings higher reward. If a preacher can keep his wits and adapt to the unfolding moment, literally crafting words not in the safety of the study, but in the heat of the moment, the effect is dramatic and palpable. People feel, in that kind of moment, a participation in the sermon. Instead of being passive receivers, they sense, and they are accurate in the sensation, that they are co-creating the sermon. If it works, they experience something quite unusual. And the preacher feels the difference too. As a preacher, you know what I'm talking about. It's where the synergy produces more than either the preacher or the audience could generate on their own. There is a sort of magic shared moment.

Yet, herein lies the danger. Anybody, believer or not, can potentially learn to do this. Pagan orators of the ancient world describe it. Hitler embodied it. Preachers more interested in personal acclaim can use the gospel to generate and seek it. In this case, the cart pulls the horse. The preacher is, honestly, more interested in the effect of the message than the message itself. There is a danger of "trafficking" in truth. This reminds me of John's sad summary of the Pharisees: "they loved the approval of men rather than the approval of God" (12:43). Preaching just for effect is a counterfeit of the real thing.

There is another way. "Preaching by ear" is humble. It means speaking with less artifice. It means speaking firsthand truth. It means sharing the spotlight with the hearers. It means being sacrificially vulnerable. It is risky, yes—but not in pursuit of glory. It actually focuses on the hearers and the message so much that a beautiful self-forgetfulness emerges. It pursues the good of the congregation more than position, polish, power, or prestige. It is in this direction we will aim—to find ourselves less automatic, less contrived, and more open in our preaching.

On Perfectly Balanced Vulnerability

I just finished perusing the latest copy of a popular pastoral journal. Its theme was (and if you read pastoral journals at all, you'll recognize the regularity of the theme) what makes a pastor fit to lead. In it I read the advice of multiple mentors. Most of them spent their time doing two things: recommending a more honest and vulnerable pulpit, while simultaneously warning about the danger of being too vulnerable. Most of us preachers, scared already at the thought of showing weakness in the pulpit, will hear enough in the warning to justify our typically overly cautious approach. Nobody, they tell us, wants to hear about the preacher's life every week. What a relief. Because I don't want to tell it every week.

And so the expectation that we be more real becomes ever greater and ever more daunting to pull off with perfect balance. I know of no way to keep this mythical balance. The only way I know to become an authentic preacher is to make mistakes doing it. If we could do it perfectly, it wouldn't be very authentic.

Preaching by ear is a move toward authenticity in the preacher.

It is the conviction that in some sense, the sermon will always implicate the preacher. The actual life and character of the preacher will always be the governor on the sermon. We cannot preach what we have not experienced. Or, rather, we can. We've all done it. But there is a cost. A sense of distance creeps in. Less eye contact. More temptation to keep repeating the obvious. Less compassion. A slightly scolding tone. Maybe we substitute strong words to cover our own nagging sense of unworthiness. We're aware, at some level, this advice we're throwing out has no sense of punch or passion to it. But we don't know how to get it. So we just keep talking until we can close in prayer.

If you learn to preach by ear, chances are people will think you're a better preacher. It's very normal to want to be a better preacher. It's very normal to want them to like you, even admire you. But that should not be the reason to learn. It should start with a conviction that you will preach nothing that you haven't wrestled with yourself. That you will ignore no problem that plagues you and advocate no solution you haven't personally tested. That you will speak from firsthand failure and firsthand discovery. That you will not mooch ideas from other people, or Scripture itself, and pass them along disconnected from your own life. Your life will inform every text even as the text informs your life. You will internalize and swallow the truth until it leaks out in ways you can't contain. You will feel the freedom of loving the highest things and calling people to that high love in words that tumble out unexpectedly and, at times, even awkwardly. But you will be speaking no longer theory, but practice. And that will make all the difference.

Preaching by Ear

If you're a musician, you know what playing by ear involves. You know how a person can hear the music as they play it and migrate around the keyboard or frets or strings without recourse to written notes. Many of these gifted performers can't even read music at all. On the other end, there are those who play proficiently only with the steady guidance sheet music provides. They can't imagine playing with nothing but an internal sense of where to go next. It would be, for them, like exploring without so much as a map. Some rare musicians can operate in either world, as comfortable reading and interpreting someone else's notations as they are launching off on their own rhythm and chord progressions.

The Literary Sermon

This metaphor provides us with a starting place for our adventure in preaching. Since the invention of the printing press and the resulting push toward widespread literacy, composition has been the key to preaching. The preparation of our notes is our foremost homiletic task. We think of the sermon as something that lives outside of us, as if the sermon itself was in this outline or that manuscript. It is something that is "there": on the desk or in a folder in the car (as sheet music might be for the musician). The notes are, at varying levels, necessary for the delivery of the sermon, and when preparation of the notes is finished, the sermon is ready. This is what we'll call the literary approach.

The Orally Driven Sermon

Other preachers, especially those before the widespread influence of the printing press upon communication thought of the sermon differently. Premodern preachers tended to view the sermon as something internally propelled. The sermon was more "inside" the preacher and could come out in a variety of ways, depending on the setting. To these preachers, the sermon could no more live on a desk than could an emotion like love or a concept like truth or a parade, battle, or argument. The sermon wasn't a thing. It was an event. It was sourced in sacred text, forged in reflection and integrative thinking, crafted orally, and delivered extemporaneously. It wasn't finished until it was preached to a live audience who had power to shape its unfolding. To resort to the metaphor again, it was preached "by ear" more than "by note."

This is hard to grasp when all we've ever been exposed to are highly literary models of preaching. From our earliest efforts we've been trained to start and end in literacy. Our research begins in the Bible itself and quickly moves toward literary mentoring via commentaries, lexicons, and blogs. Reading is our primary mode for preparation. Studying for a sermon is framed entirely as a literary process. We decipher a core message from the text and then begin to structure that idea, to illustrate it and apply it. To do this we make recourse to what has become almost the sole tool of homiletic organization: the outline. That's what we're all trying to do each week: get it into an outline. From there, some of us will write out the entire sermon. Others will just try to get as familiar as possible with the outline. But all this can be done alone and in silence, leaving us unprepared for the shared and spoken moment that will occur on Sunday.

What Sunday Requires of Us

From start to finish this has been a literary task. Reading and writing have been the dominant, maybe even the only, skills necessary. Ironically, however, on Sunday those skills won't be altogether helpful since the sermon has to morph, like it or not, from notes to event. If the preacher was going to distribute a copy of his sermon to be quietly read by the congregation each Sunday, then literacy would be the perfect kind of preparation. In fact, it would be the only kind of preparation necessary.

But what we sometimes fail to grasp is that the delivery of a sermon is a primarily oral event. So to prepare in pure literacy for an oral event seems to be a mismatch between skills and setting. It leads us to wonder if there might be another kind of preparation that is more fitting to the eventual outcome. In other words, since we're going to end up speaking anyway, why not get there way before Sunday morning? That way we'll be preparing for the actual thing we're going to do. Otherwise, it seems we're like musicians preparing for a concert by studying and writing sheet music; or like football players preparing for Sunday by going over and over the playbook. While the playbook is a necessary part, there is a greater need to be stretching, blocking, throwing, and catching—the skills actually employed in the game.

Old and New

What we're talking about here in oral preparation and delivery of a sermon might sound new and different. But I'll try to demonstrate that it's actually very old. It's always difficult to see the arbitrary nature of our habits. After all, we've been doing them so long and so unconsciously we may not even see that our habitual way is only one way to approach a task. If we've been driving a certain way to work for ten years, all the other options may not even occur to us. Since preaching has been dominated by literacy for at least three hundred years, it's hard to imagine it any other way. But the literary way used to be the new way. And we're used to always thinking of the newer way as the better way. Typing on a laptop instead of typewriter is obviously easier. In fact it's hard to see any downside to giving up typewriters. So we tend to frame older ways as inferior. But sometimes they're not.

Today we see recent technology affecting preaching in a variety of ways. It's great to be able to do research online. In some ways, this is progress. But every technological advance exacts some kind of toll. The Internet has unquestionably made more resources available to more people. But it has also had a privatizing effect, since I can now consult a virtually infinite number of resources all alone and in silence. I need other people less and less.

Long before the Internet, another invention shook the communicative world in similar ways. Information sharing took quantum steps forward when the printing press entered the scene. But like the Internet it also introduced and fostered a private means to acquire information and a way to externalize thought onto page or screen. All advances in literacy have a tendency to separate thoughts from the thinker and facilitate private reading. In the ancient world, even reading was done aloud and with others. Ideas were shaped in community and shared by a speaker from the inside out. That's the world to which we'll turn as we consult perhaps the most influential of all the church fathers, St. Augustine.

2

THE WISE PREACHER

Augustine's Homiletic

> *For no one may benefit another with that which*
> *he does not have himself.*
>
> St. Augustine, *On Christian Doctrine*

I was walking down the hill from what we call "the cabin" to our actual church building when it happened. It was the middle of winter, which in our context means a fire needs to be lit in the stove that heats the simple building where our youth group meets on Sunday mornings. I don't mind lighting the fire. I get there very early, at least an hour or so before anybody else arrives. Lighting the fire gives me a chance to be alone for a while in the predawn chill. Normally it takes a half hour before any warmth rises from the stove, so I stand there rubbing my hands together and mentally going over my sermon. Some mornings I even preach it to the assembled couches and foosball table.

On this particular morning I was walking the hundred yards between the cabin and our main building, snow crunching under my feet. Sky aglow, the sun was just starting to get up the nerve to rise. Unexpectedly, I heard a voice, inaudible, yet clear. A voice from inside. "Where are you in this?"

Where Are You in This?

I knew what the voice meant. The voice meant the sermon. The one I had just been running through my head. It wanted to know if I had tried the things I would be talking about, or if the sermon was only hypothetically true. I didn't want to answer even though I was the only one who would have heard me. The answer was, "I don't know." The fuller answer was, "Why do you keep badgering me about this? Leave me alone."

I can't parse out that voice. I don't know where my conscience ended and the Holy Spirit began. I'm not even sure I can reliably distinguish the two. But it was a voice. An irritating voice. In my head I answered back something like, "You know what? It's an hour before church starts. You can't seriously expect me to go back and start revising things now." But the voice didn't say anything else.

I'd like to say I heeded the voice. Went back and changed something. Or at least prayed for a direction that might be missing. But I decided to stick with what I had prepared. I reassured myself with the reminder that people don't need to hear about me every week.

Later my wife made an observation about the detached feel of the sermon, and I knew she was right. It came out okay. The ideas were there. It wasn't a disaster. But I knew I wasn't in it. My heart wasn't in it. I had a warning from someplace deep that I ignored. I'm not a sage in such things, but I know when you consciously ignore things you know to be true, no more help is forthcoming.

So we come to the issue of the preacher behind the sermon. How much do we put ourselves in? I don't think the voice demanded that I insert any particular story about myself. I think the voice just wanted to know where this truth had been tried in my life. It wanted me to be able to name that moment. To be able to feel it and describe it in a firsthand way.

It's the same issue I face as I write this chapter. Where am I in this book? It would be easy for me to pass along insights that I've studied, and easy to make a case for their history and value. But I could do all that in a very depersonalized way. I could leave myself, and my own journey, out of the book entirely. But that wouldn't be firsthand. If I'm going to write in the way I'm telling you to preach, I have to write about things that I've tried and am trying. Indeed, I tried something last week that you'll hear about later in this chapter. I'd like to say I've been doing it for years, but I haven't. But I'd like to make this more a journey of discovery than a method of sermon mastery. So I am choosing to put myself in the book so that I can tell you to put yourself in the sermon.

First Things First

St. Augustine was the Bishop of Hippo from AD 396 to 430 in the region we today call Algeria. We forget sometimes that North Africa has an eminent Christian history. As the church spread around the Mediterranean in its first two centuries, the Roman colonies on the coast, especially after Constantine's conversion, became thoroughly Christian. There were numerous notable churches in the city where Augustine ministered, and even a basilica. Hippo was a middle-class city full of tradesmen and merchants. With Rome falling and unable to defend its frontiers, Augustine died there in AD 430 while Vandals were besieging the city.[1]

Augustine was that North African bishop who, perhaps more than any other church father, sensed the timelessness of everything essential. Writing at the time of Rome's declining influence, Augustine had a confidence in truth that was greater than any particular historical setting. That's why his influence is still pervasive in every corner and branch of the Christian church and his fifth-century observations are strikingly relevant fifteen centuries later.

I don't know what you picture when you think of preaching in the ancient world. But when you read about what it was actually like inside the church during Augustine's sermons, you find it was pretty much like today. Aside from the fact that preachers often sat while they preached, all the other elements worked the same way. We have more than nine hundred of Augustine's sermons in

---

1   *Encyclopaedia Britannica Online*, s.v. "Saint Augustine," accessed May 6, 2014, http://www.britannica.com/EBchecked/topic/42902/Saint-Augustine.

written form. But it's important to note that we have them not because they were composed ahead of time, but because they were captured via shorthand as he preached. Even today he comes across as warm, funny, sarcastic, introspective, bold, and always saturated in Scripture. Though his writing is scholarly and of the highest caliber, his preaching was very down to earth and about everyday concerns of average people. He spoke in a way that reflected the world and the church of his day.

Before his conversion, Augustine was a teacher of public speaking in Milan, Italy, and made a lot of money doing it. Now, today we don't think of public speaking as a large component of our educational systems. But in his day, every educated person was trained extensively in public speaking. Many became quite proficient at it. They were trained in techniques of both composition and delivery. They learned how to achieve the standard of the day: eloquence. Eloquence described a person who could convincingly make a case with good reasons and corresponding passion.

At times Augustine demonstrated contempt for this obsession with technique. It's not that he found no value in it, but he knew that technique could easily substitute for something even more important. Listen to him carefully as he described effective speaking: "The precepts of eloquence are found to have been fulfilled . . . although the speakers did not think of them in order to be eloquent or while they were being eloquent" (*De doctrina christiana* 4.3.4).[2]

There's a lot packed into this simple observation. He redefined eloquence from something that is constructed by rules to something that flows naturally from the inside out. A good preacher, he said, will not be consumed with looking eloquent or sounding eloquent. The good preacher is consumed with the

---

2   All citations of Augustine's *De doctrina christiana* are taken from Augustine, *On Christian Doctrine*, trans. D. W. Robertson Jr. (Upper Saddle River, NJ: Prentice-Hall, 1958). Primary sources referenced in the text and some footnotes generally use English titles, but Latin titles such as *De doctrina christiana* are used in parenthetical citations.

truth of the message, which fuels a sort of unschooled or natural eloquence that is self-forgetful.

Think of what this means. Eloquence is not something we seek. It's something that is the by-product of loving the truth, not of careful planning and structuring. It's where we forget how we sound and how we look and are carried along by a different energy. We end up eloquent organically, not by planning. But that's a tall order. Could we possibly be so "into" our message that we forget ourselves? How would that work?

As the quotation at the beginning of this chapter demonstrates, it starts with a personal ownership of the message. We cannot effectively pass on to others what we don't possess ourselves. But the things we do possess, things that have become native to us, we can pass along quite naturally, dare I say it, effortlessly.

For example, if I asked you to tell a familiar story from your past—say, your first date, or your favorite movie or meal—you could speak quite naturally about such things. You wouldn't have to prepare or outline or structure your thoughts. You wouldn't have to worry about how the words might come out. These things are very close to you. So close that you can get caught up in the story and forget about how you're saying it.

No doubt this happens when you're preaching at certain points. You might put on your outline "Truck Story." You're not worried about how you're going to express the story because it's so close to you. Other things, however, are not so close. Things that are more distant from us, or abstract, are harder to express naturally. I can talk about birdwatching in a general way, but because I've never been personally involved in birdwatching, anything I say on the subject will have a sense of distance. No matter how hard I work to make it sound personal, nothing can change the fact that I've never really watched birds. I can't manufacture that out of willpower or research.

Our fluency suffers to the extent that something is less familiar, or secondhand. Augustine simply says that the things we speak about should be possessed as something firsthand. When we possess them, we have the ability to forget ourselves while speaking. And something else happens. Augustine says we'll embody many of the principles of eloquence without even realizing it.

This is the beauty of putting first things first. He explains that some things are to be enjoyed and loved (*De doctrina christiana*, 1.3.3). These are the highest things, ultimately God himself. Other things are to be used to get us toward those highest things. We get into trouble when we love things that should be used; or when we use things that should be loved. Let's make the jump to preaching.

If we love anything more than the truth of our message, we have elevated a lower thing above the higher thing.[3] If we love the construction and preaching of sermons more than the truth in the sermon, we have flipped something on its ear. We are then elevating the act of preaching over the message of the sermon. We are "using" something that should be loved: trafficking in truth for some other purpose.

Loving Truth More Than Its Expression

If we're honest, we've all done this. We've used the sermon to show off either our skill or our scholarship. Graciously, God uses us even in the midst of this kind of self-service. But in this scenario we won't be able to be self-forgetful. We'll be aware of how we're doing even in the midst of the sermon. We'll be evaluating ourselves and thinking either, "I think they're with me and it feels great" or "I think I've lost them and it feels terrible." Either way, we're self-aware. Our biggest concern is how we're doing. This kills our firsthand connection to the message and the audience, and introduces a competing concern that siphons off a good deal of our attentiveness from others toward ourselves. The message and the people deserve our full attention. To the extent that we lose track of ourselves, to that extent we can be naturally eloquent.

Philosopher Martin Buber tells the story of his youth in his

---

3   Augustine calls this loving words more than the things the words point to. Our theological words are pointers to the "real" reality. They're just tools. We use words, but we don't enjoy them or love them. "He is a slave to a sign who uses or worships a significant thing without knowing what it signifies" (*De doctrina christiana* 3.9.13).

grandparents' horse stables. As an eleven-year-old he had a favorite mare he would visit daily. It was a great joy to him to have this giant, gentle beast offer her mane for his small hand to stroke, and to feel the power and pulse of that friendship was exhilarating. It was the excitement of being so close to something so powerful and so different; another being that could not be controlled. There was a vitality and magic in each visit. I'll let him tell the rest. "But once . . . it struck me about the stroking, what fun it gave me, and suddenly I became conscious of my hand. The game went on as before, but something had changed. It was no longer the same thing."[4]

The only thing that had changed was self-consciousness. Being aware of himself in a way that made the uniqueness, the otherness, of the horse disappear. Instead of there being two beings, there was only himself. Something similar happens when we watch ourselves preach. We lose the others. In terms of our attentiveness, everyone else dissolves, at least for a while. We also lose our essential connection to the truth we're speaking. We become suddenly alone in a full room.

I don't think it's possible to purge our self-interest or self-awareness from preaching. It will always be present to some degree. It's impossible to stand up in front of people without a single concern over how we appear. But we can, at least, be aware of this insecurity that threatens what Augustine calls true eloquence. We have to be very aware of the possibility of doing a good thing with a bad motive.[5] He argues that our own personal lives have much greater bearing on our sermon's success than any "grandness in eloquence."[6] The life of the preacher is prior to the sermon. He even admits that others might benefit from a secondhand sermon,

---

4   Martin Buber, *Between Man and Man* (London: Routledge Classics, 2002), 27.

5   Augustine says, "For in all things of this kind, we are to be commended or reprimanded, not because of the nature of things we use, but because of the motive in using them and the way in which they are desired" (*De doctrina christiana* 3.7.18).

6   Ibid., 4.27.59.

but that the practice is dangerous to the preacher's own soul. This refers to when we talk confidently about things we don't really know about. We're bluffing our way along, hoping someone won't call the bluff. They probably won't. After all, we're saying true things. But Augustine says we're cut off from natural eloquence with this kind of distance between ourselves and the thing we're talking about.

A Better Way

Augustine also has a vision for a better way. Referring to those who were attempting to memorize long passages of Scripture without really knowing the meaning, he describes something much more authentic. Those are the wiser preachers who "remember the words less well, but who look into the heart of the Scriptures with the *eye of their own heart*" (*De doctrina christiana* 4.6.7; emphasis mine).

"Eye of their own heart." What does that mean? Remember when I mentioned speaking about birdwatching, but only in a general way? Theology can be the same. We all know our correct position on our basic theology. We can define it, explain it, compare it. But the eye of our heart has more than that in mind. Our theology must be experienced in our own lives to unlock the firsthand sense in our sermons. Our own spiritual experience and maturity will necessarily be the governor on our sermons. We can't take people somewhere we've never been.

This is where our emotions play a role in preaching. So much of sermon preparation and delivery is limited to thinking. True thoughts about true things. But, as the apostle James says, demons can acknowledge what's true (2:19). Emotion, or what Augustine calls the "eye of their own heart" requires personal engagement. Feeling. I think that's all that voice was saying to me that morning. Has your heart's eye digested this passage? Or are you just passing along secondhand truth?

Augustine has one more test to evaluate motives in preaching. If we truly love the message and the people more than the preaching, he said we'll be fueled more by time spent in prayer before preaching than in our conventional sorts of research and outlining.[7] Many of us don't do very well on that test. Truth be told, we often think that come Sunday, it's good content and good structuring that will be the most helpful.

Augustine describes a piety that precedes preaching. Piety that produces grounded eloquence. There is an anecdote about him visiting one of the churches in his parish. As bishop, he was the natural guest preacher on Sunday. In those days the churches used a simple lectionary so that every preacher prepared from an agreed-upon text. When getting up to read the text for which Augustine had prepared, a young lector made a mistake and read the wrong passage (which happened to be Psalm 51, on repentance). Instead of considering it a mistake, the bishop took it as divine direction to preach on repentance instead of what he had planned. It's interesting to read the account and see the gracious way he handled the entire situation.[8] This is the kind of grounding he not only recommended, but lived out. Even more than preparation for any given sermon, Augustine calls us to an ear for Scripture that looks beyond words to spiritual realities that reside within the preacher. There's a self-forgetfulness here and a trust in something other than our own abilities.

Becoming a Theologian First

Michael Pasquarello in *Sacred Rhetoric* calls for the priority of theology over homiletics. The best preachers in the history of the church, he argues, were theologians before they were preachers.[9] One did not study in order to preach. Study was

---

7   Augustine says, "If he is at all able, and to the extent that he is able, more through the piety of his prayers than through the skill of his oratory, so that, praying for himself and for those whom he is to address, he is a petitioner before he is a speaker. When the hour in which he is to speak approaches, before he begins to preach, he should raise his thirsty soul to God in order that he may give forth what he shall drink, or pour out what shall fill him" (ibid., 4.15.32).

8   Sermon 352 is the happy accident that resulted. Augustine, *Treatises (341–400) on Various Subjects* (New York: New City Press, 1995), 137.

9   Michael Pasquarello III, *Sacred Rhetoric: Preaching as a Theological and*

inherently good and necessary, regardless of outcome or expression. That the study made its way "out" in grounded sermons was natural and fitting, but not the stimulus for the labor involved.

Pasquarello calls us to study for the love of God and truth, not for what will preach. In a world of pragmatic preparation and shoddy theological grounding, his call sounds oddly inefficient. Most of us would be uncomfortable with the title "theologian." We're more comfortable saying things like, "I'm no theologian, but here's what I think about . . ." But what if we are supposed to be theologians first? I don't mean the stereotypical bookish sage who can read four languages. I just mean a pastor who meditates on things that may never fit into a sermon. Things that are just true and honest and beautiful. Things seen with what Augustine calls "the eye of our hearts."

Augustine on Using Pagans

This priority of truth over its expression goes way back to the ancient world. Even before Augustine, pagan philosophers and educators argued the same point. But to what extent can we use pagans as mentors for preaching? Augustine faced this same issue in the transition between the pagan world and the emerging Christian culture.[10] Though not slavishly bound to rhetoric and well aware of its propensity for manipulation and deceit, he nonetheless recognized its value in defending and propagating the faith as well, quoting as easily from Cicero

---

Pastoral Practice of the Church (Grand Rapids: Eerdmans, 2005). Pasquarello surveys Augustine, Gregory the Great, St. Benedict, Bernard of Clairvaux, Bonadventure, Aquinas, Erasmus, Latimer, Luther, and Calvin looking for homiletic grounding uninfluenced by contemporary practice.

10 Augustinian scholar John Schaeffer summarizes the church father's response (who himself was a former pagan): "As a rhetor himself, he knew the advantages that his training conferred, but he also rejected the applause-seeking artificiality that he thought characterized many of his contemporaries." John Schaeffer, "The Dialectic of Orality and Literacy: The Case of Book 4 of Augustine's *De doctrina Christiana*," *PMLA* 111, no. 5: 1136. (*PMLA* is the journal of the Modern Language Association of America.)

and Virgil as from Scripture.[11] Here his famous classification of all truth as divine provides a particularly fitting analysis.

> But we should not think that we ought not to learn literature because Mercury is said to be its inventor, nor that because the pagans dedicated temples to Justice and Virtue, and adored in stones what should be performed in the heart, we should therefore avoid justice and virtue. Rather, every good and true Christian should understand that wherever he may find truth, it is his Lord's. (*De doctrina christiana* 2.18.28)

In saying all truth is the Lord's, Augustine, while prioritizing scriptural content over pagan, seems oddly at home in the world, and unthreatened by what might be discovered therein. Where it helps, let it help.

Familiarity with classical speaking theory does help us in a variety of ways. Whether or not we agree with dead pagans is, at this point, beside the point. Approve or disapprove, pagan theorists demonstrated explicitly how communication actually worked in the ancient world. It is precisely that communicative context and no other that produced the speech, preserved by writing, that became Scripture. Peeling back our more modern and literary orientation we can see the oral foundations to the written Word of God and perhaps "hear" and "speak" from it as we might not otherwise. Do ancient pagans understand the heart of our faith? No, not if we mean full and personal understanding. So there is a limit on what they can teach us. They are operating from what theologians called

---

11 Augustine was not alone in this dual intellectual agility. "In Clement there are *more* references to Greek literature, to Homer, Plato, Aristotle, Euripides, Chrysippus, Plutarch, and other Greek authors than to the Bible. Yet there is a difference. Clement cites Greek literature to illustrate a point, to give flourish to an argument, to delight and amuse his readers. When he cites Scripture, there is a sense of discovery, that something extraordinary is to be learned from its pages, that it is not one book among many." Robert Louis Wilken, *The Spirit of Early Christian Thought: Seeking the Face of God* (New Haven, CT: Yale University Press, 2003), 57.

common grace.[12] It is the ability to make valid observations about the world without having been converted. Non-Christians make startling inventions and observations all the time as a result of a marred, but still functioning image of God. Because of their setting in the time of the early church, such people offer us things we simply can't gain from any contemporary voices.

Contemporary instructors in preaching cannot help but be influenced by the pervasive, sometimes dominant, role of literacy in contemporary homiletics. Try as we might, it is difficult to forget what we already know and change what we already do. We teach as we were taught. But by listening to the insights from classical practitioners, we gain otherwise impossible access to a world where tongue and text worked in complementary fashion, and where the Word of God came to the church of God with all the fervor of an orally conditioned setting. With Augustine's introduction, we now turn toward Aristotle, the father of all subsequent models of public speaking, and a pagan with surprising insight into our world of preaching.

---

12 For more on common grace from a Reformed perspective, see Abraham Kuyper, *Common Grace*, trans. Nelson D. Kloosterman and Ed M. van der Maas, ed. Jordan J. Ballor and Stephen J. Grabill, 3 vols. (Grand Rapids: CLP Academic, 2013–).

3

BALONEY

Why We Trust Some Speakers and Dismiss Others

It is not true, as some writers assume on their treatises on rhetoric, that the personal goodness revealed by the speaker contributes nothing to his power of persuasion; on the contrary his character must almost be called the most effective means of persuasion he possesses.

Aristotle, *Rhetoric*

When I was in my last year of seminary I found myself looking in earnest for the place where I would start to live out my calling. Maybe you remember such a time. When you're at that point and feeling a little urgency about getting it settled, you find yourself surprisingly open to new opportunities. So when a man arrived on campus interviewing potential church planters, I decided to give it a shot. This was not something I had ever contemplated, but the more I thought about it, the more open I tried to become.

I took a personal inventory and then sat down for the interview. The man asked a lot of questions, most of which I don't remember. I do remember the key question, however: "Why do you want to plant a church?" I guess the most honest response would have been something about my need for a job as opposed to my plans to reach a community. But I was trying to make a real effort in the right direction. So I sincerely came up with my best set of convictions about why churches need to be planted and why I felt a desire to do so.

The man listened patiently. But then he said something that

surprised me. He said he didn't think I really wanted to plant a church. But how could this be? I had just told him why I wanted to plant a church. I had good reasons. I thought I was fairly articulate. But he said something about it being unconvincing. That I didn't sound like I really wanted to do it. I had almost convinced myself. So why would he say such a thing?

It turned out he was right. Later, I understood. This man had learned to look for telltale signs of passion and drive. Although I was earnest, I couldn't pull off fabricating on the fly something he was looking for deep in one's character. More than my words, he was listening and looking for conviction. He knew that without it, I'd probably hurt myself and others trying to plant a church. Thank goodness he listened at more than a surface level.

Here's what's important. We all have this ability. We've all learned to discern whether people really mean what they say. Speech reveals us. I suppose that's why being more extemporaneous is so threatening. We might say something wrong. People might see more of the real us. A tight outline, a well-crafted manuscript can hide some of that. But not when you're live in the moment. Whether we like it or not, whether we deny it or not, people see things and hear things that reveal other deeper things.

Personal Ethos

In this chapter we're going to talk about what Aristotle called *ethos*. Ethos is that ability a speaker has to be authentic in the act of speaking. As author of the systematic *Rhetoric* in 335 BC, Aristotle stands uncontested as the foremost authority on public speaking at a time when public speaking was at a very highly developed stage. That's right. People were better at it in the ancient world than we are today because the printing press had not yet changed the way we communicate. We'll uncover this thoroughly in chapter 6. But what does classical theory on public speaking have to do with preaching? At a very foundational level, they're both concerned with persuasion. In fact, that's Aristotle's fundamental description of rhetoric: the art of persuasion. He acknowledged that most of the things we must decide in life don't come with scientific precision. We have to decide the best course of action based on probability, not certainty.[1] This is the science of how people hold their views and how they change them. In the ancient world, they called this science "rhetoric." Rhetoric helps us advocate the best course of action among many possibilities. Do you see the overlap with preaching?

You may not think of yourself as persuading when you preach. But if we are trying to affect attitudes and behavior, we are persuading. We are asking people to view something differently or change the way they respond to situations. We want to bring people to a point of decision.

This is the ground of homiletics. Our sermons are about transcendent, universal truths. Truths that are bigger than we are, and truths we cannot control or create. Truths that go on, with or without our consent. Yet our access to those truths is not with scientific precision, and that by divine design. What Aristotle called contingency, we could call faith. God intentionally leaves things muddy enough that it requires some stepping beyond empirical knowledge to participate. Faith and rhetoric go hand in glove, for rhetoric is most at home in the world of probability, the world of contingency.

This is a world that, while old, is ironically relevant. Borrowing from premoderns like Aristotle equips us to handle challenges from both relativists who say there is no objective truth, and hip-pocket

---

1   Aristotle said, "Most of the things about which we make decisions, and into which therefore we inquire, present us with alternative possibilities. For it is about our actions that we deliberate and inquire, and all our actions have a contingent character; hardly any of them are determined by necessity." *Rhetorica* 1.2 in *The Rhetoric and the Poetics of Aristotle*, trans. W. Rhys Roberts and Ingram Bywater, resp. (1954; repr., New York: Random House, 1984), 1357^a 24. The introduction to this edition explains that along with the primary source book and chapter numbers are "four-digit numbers in the outer margins—for example 1365^b—[that] refer to pages in Immanuel Bekker's edition (1837) of the Greek text of Aristotle. The one- and two-digit numbers in the outer margins are the line numbers on a particular page of the Bekker edition" (xxxi). All subsequent citations of the primary source and Bekker's numbering refer to this edition, and the Latin title *Rhetorica* is used in parenthetical citations except above.

defenders of Christianity who try to prove things that are simply not provable.[2] The ancient world and our world both run largely on faith. This is close to what the apostle Paul describes as his persuasive method in 1 Corinthians 2:1–5:

> And when I came to you, brethren, I did not come with superiority of speech or of wisdom, proclaiming to you the testimony of God. For I determined to know nothing among you except Jesus Christ, and Him crucified. I was with you in weakness and in fear and in much trembling, and my message and my preaching were not in persuasive words of wisdom, but in demonstration of the Spirit and of power, so that your faith would not rest on the wisdom of men, but on the power of God.[3]

Persuasion was central for Aristotle's rhetoric since he defined rhetoric as "observing in any given case the available means of persuasion" (*Rhetorica* 1.2; 1355^b 26). Yet persuasion works differently in different communicative settings. Aristotle's means to persuasion are summarized in three categories: *logos* (rationale), *pathos* (emotion), and *ethos* (credibility).[4] If we attempt to apply Aristotle to preaching, it makes sense to focus on ethos since it is the factor most directly linked to environments where the speaker is working in an area of shared values. In other words, if a speaker is working with a hostile audience, then perhaps reasoning or emotion would play greater roles. But when the gathered audience shares basic values, it's not information they need, but motivation

---

2   This is not to imply that the empirically observable is more ontologically "real." For more on the complex relationship of science and theology, including a defense of theology's nonempirical ontology, see Cambridge physicist and Anglican priest John Polkinghorne's *Exploring Reality: The Intertwining of Science and Theology* (New Haven, CT: Yale University Press, 2006).

3   All biblical quotations are from the New American Standard Bible (NASB).

4   Aristotle also spelled out three primary communicative environments: forensic (legal), deliberative (legislative), and epideictic (ceremonial) (see *Rhetorica* 1.2).

or inspiration. This is a factor of ethos.

It is only a few pages into book 1 of *Rhetoric* that we encounter Aristotle's first mention of ethos. Predictably, it is listed along with its two counterparts: pathos and logos, but listed first among the three: "The first kind depends on the personal character of the speaker; the second on putting the audience into a certain frame of mind; the third on the proof, or apparent proof, provided by the words of the speech itself" (1.2; 1356ª 2).

It is ethos, he admitted, that carries the most persuasive force.[5] He then elaborated on what he means by personal character. First he stressed that ethos is working during the speech event so as to "make us think him credible." Strictly speaking, he was not concerned with a speaker's reputation or pedigree outside the speech. The crucial dynamic Aristotle sought to isolate is what the audience perceives coming from the actual speech event. Outside competence is harder for an audience to access than what they see and hear right in front of them. The man interviewing me as a church planter was not looking at my résumé, but listening between my words. It was "live" me that revealed the truth.

Consider the difference between the following rhetorical strategies. In one case a preacher exhorts his audience to be honest at all times and extols, with great passion, the virtue and necessity of being honest. In another case the preacher says very little about honesty, yet discloses a fault about himself, say, his tendency to be lazy or to lose his temper. In the first case, the subject is honesty. But in the second case, the sermon actually is *itself* honest.[6] The congregation can sense the difference and will grant ethos to the second preacher more readily than the first (who will be perceived as merely stating the obvious).

This acknowledgment of the power of personal character in the midst of speaking distinguishes Aristotle's sense from later descriptions of ethos that flow from a person's character outside the

---

5   Although Aristotle's personal favorite was logos, he concedes that ethos "may almost be called the most effective means of persuasion he possesses" (*Rhetorica* 1.2; 1356ª 13).

6   I owe this illuminating distinction to a particularly helpful interaction with Dr. Calvin Troup while in my studies at Duquesne University.

speech (most notably, Quintilian in the next chapter).[7] Aristotle made it clear that, at least for the point under discussion, he was only referring to a very specific kind of ethos. It's not hard to picture how a preacher's internal character would improve the sermon. Augustine has established that. But how would credibility emerge from the speech event itself? How does a preacher build credibility in the midst of the sermon?

Homiletic Ethos

Let's take a deeper look at why Aristotle made such a point of this.[8] In terms of "live" ethos, every speech starts at ground zero and must build from scratch. This means when we get up to preach, people have built-in baloney detectors. Whether we know this crowd well or are speaking as a guest, we only have a couple minutes to make a first impression. Aristotle stated that this first impression leaks out of us. People have a way of making a judgment on whether we come across as sincere or with a sense of distance or duplicity. They will sense this from within and may not be able to put words to it. What are they looking for? We'll distill it down to five factors: reputation, vision, authority, good reasons, and shared time.[9] All five have some bearing upon the preacher since these are how an audience decides to trust us or not.

Reputation

What personality do I bring to the pulpit? Am I speaking consistently with my personality, or am I acting differently, perhaps

---

7   This seems to be a significant point since Aristotle goes out of his way to describe an ethos "achieved by what the speaker says, not by what people think of his character before he begins to speak" (1.2; 1356ᵃ 9).

8   Aristotle is not denying that a person's reputation outside the speech can affect ethos. But that kind of reputation is not working as an artistic proof from within the speech. He is concerned with ethos produced by the speech event.

9   I'm borrowing these categories from Aristotelian scholar Dale Sullivan in his article on ethos in the sermonic environment. See Dale L. Sullivan, "The Ethos of Epideictic Encounter," *Philosophy and Rhetoric* 26, no. 2 (1993): 117.

with a preaching persona? When people talk to me before or
after the sermon, am I the same person? Preachers who take on a
different persona (tone of voice and mannerism) when they get up
to preach lose credibility. The audience catches the duplicity and
doesn't trust the "imposter."

Vision

Vision is remembering that the message preached comes from
outside of the speaker. The seer, the prophet, and the preacher
announce a message coming from another place, from heaven itself.
Remembering this serves as a safeguard against the hubris of public
speaking as grandstanding. Hear Paul on this perspective: "[God] has
committed to us the word of reconciliation. Therefore, we are ambas-
sadors for Christ, as though God were making an appeal through
us; we beg you on behalf of Christ, be reconciled to God" (2 Cor.
5:19–20). So the question for the preacher is this: Do I give the sense
that my message comes from outside myself? Is there a sense of
announcement or declaration? Do I really see myself as the conduit
for God's message, or is it actually more my own bright ideas?

Authority

Authority is the sense of confidence that transmits from a
speaker to an audience. Can I speak with authority from God or do
I pander? Am I more interested in seeking audience approval than
I am telling the truth? While we might think we gain credibility by
playing to our audience, the opposite actually occurs. People respect
someone who challenges them and questions the status quo. They
can sense when someone is trying to campaign for their approval.

Good Reasons

The ethos of the speaker is energized with good reasons. There is
no need to be shy about being persuasive. Being openly persuasive
shows respect for an audience's ability to reason and choose. So
besides being authoritative, do I also supplement my declarations
with good reasons? Clear and winsome reasoning adds credibility.

Think about your last ten sermons. Were you trying to move

anyone? Bring them to a point of decision? Persuade? Informational sermons don't move anyone. We have to offer good reasons that demonstrate why a person should change something. Preachers who have a conviction on where people should go will have a natural desire to see change.

Shared Time

This last dynamic speaks of a shared timelessness between audience and speaker. This just means a sense of union between preacher and audience—a togetherness. This is what we mean when we say a certain audience was or wasn't "with" me. Literally speaking, both audiences were "there." But sometimes they can be there, but not there.[10] Aristotle's description of the preaching environment is concerned with the present (as opposed to the past or the future). Sharing time in such a way that the congregation forgets about time is the idea here. We all know that a ten-minute sermon can be "long," while a forty-minute sermon can be "short." It is not about actual time, but perceived or shared time.

Shared time can be illustrated right now in your reading. As you progress through this chapter, you are either aware or not aware of how close you are to the end. If your point of attention is fixed toward finishing this chapter, you can almost now "cross it off" and feel good about your progress. You're getting through this book. You will finish it. Yes. But I have bad news for you. The goal is not to finish this book or any book. There is nothing virtuous about finishing a book. Yet, to be honest, that's often what I'm doing when I read. I want to know how I'm doing toward my goal. I feel good about finishing a section (as if that meant anything in real life). But every once in a while, I lose myself in a book. I turn a page and find that

---

10   Sullivan argues that this forges a phenomenological unity between preacher and congregation, an important factor when we think about preaching's ability to foster community. "Things that are consubstantial share substance, and, if in some metaphysical sense, we can say that those who share a common mental or spiritual space also share a common substance, we begin to experience ethos as consubstantiality" (ibid., 127).

the chapter is over and I didn't see it coming. Or the sermon is over, and I was still hoping for more. A more than "cross-offable" dynamic is in play. If only our sermons could be like that.

Pertinent questions for preachers include: Do I address the present tense? Do I make the audience part of the sermon? Does the sermon adapt to the events and people of the room? Is there a timelessness in the room, or are people glancing at their watches? Have we, in any sense, lost track of time?

Isn't it surprising how insightful an old dead pagan can be? Writing and thinking within a century or so after Ezra and Nehemiah were trying to rebuild the Jewish colony under Persian rule, we see how carefully and thoroughly Aristotle addresses these communicative issues. Before the age of electricity and way before the printing press, speaking was more important than writing. People spoke first, and then later wrote down what was noteworthy. Eventually that order would reverse. People wrote first, and then used the writing to structure the speech. If we are to recover some of that old authenticity, that old ethos, we'll have to put away some of our technology and concentrate on the vital link between heart and mouth. How did Jesus say it? "For the mouth speaks out of that which fills the heart" (Matt. 12:34). Ethos is the revealing of the heart by the mouth.

Jesus addresses a lot of these concerns in the early part of Matthew 23. He tells the crowds and his disciples that the scribes and Pharisees put themselves in the position of Mosaic authority and thus they are to do what the religious leaders say. Because what they *say* is not the problem. Their official positions on things are tolerably accurate. They just don't *live out* their own advice. He says it with spot-on simplicity: "they say, but they don't do." (v. 3). That, says Jesus, is the problem. Their lack of ethos outside their speeches eroded their ethos from within the speech. The two are always linked.

So let's apply that to ourselves. It's easy to have the correct position on things. The right doctrine, the right conviction, even the subtle sense of balance when we know we might err in either extreme. That's not the hard part. The hard part is living up to

our own advice and admitting we fail at our own standards. The
Pharisees lacked ethos because there was an essential discrepancy
between what is claimed and what is lived. That discrepancy,
as long as it goes unacknowledged, kills both credibility and
authenticity. We can only give untested advice, like a travel agent
who can tell you all about Australia, but has never been there.

We need to travel to the places we describe to others. It should
not be hypothetical truths we announce. We gain credibility when
we talk about things we know firsthand in ways that reveal our own
experience with it. Yes, credibility emerges from within the speech.
That was Aristotle's point. But in the next chapter we're going
to hear the other side of ethos from a man who, while familiar
with Aristotle, lived about five hundred years later. His name is
Marcus Fabius Quintilianus (Quintilian for short). While you've
probably never heard of him, he was the foremost communication
scholar in the Roman world. What Quintilian laid down as most
important became the foundation of what we call today a liberal
arts education. Quintilian said ethos will never have a chance to
emerge from the speech unless it already lives in the speaker. That's
the topic of the next chapter.

4

QUINTILIAN

A Surprising Preaching Tutor

I am convinced that no one can be an orator who is not a good man, and even if anyone could, I should be unwilling that he should be.

Quintilian, *Institutes of Oratory*

Since I was a pastor's kid and in church almost constantly, it was natural that I learned a lot of Bible verses. I was raised in a day when kids memorized a lot from the Bible. It seems we were always learning verses. Usually it was to earn points for something. But we "oralized" a lot of Scripture in those days. My dad used to coax us through memory verses in Wednesday night prayer meeting. He would say them out loud and then we'd all say them along with him. Just being there every week planted dozens of verses that rattled around in my head. Was I old enough to understand what I was memorizing? Not yet. But God was showing me something about how the Word of God used to reside with people in bygone eras.

Becoming Oral on Accident

In junior high school I found another opportunity to stretch in the verbal arts: Bible quizzing. I'm not certain, but it's a pretty safe bet that this anomaly in Christian subculture has largely fallen into disuse. Yet when and where I grew up, Bible quizzing was big.

The concept is fairly simple. You memorized as much of a given New Testament book as you could. Then you went to weekly practice sessions where you sat on electric pads. The equipment had a sort of Soviet-era simplicity. The first one to jump off their seat lit a corresponding light on a small display panel prompting the light judge to bark out something like, "Three Northwest!" Hopefully that was you and it was your chance to advance to the microphone. You then had thirty seconds to provide an answer. If you were really on your game, you jumped before the question was finished. In this case you had the added drama of finishing the question before supplying the answer. If you hit it right, the quizmaster would call out affirmingly "correct question," which always bolstered your confidence to proceed.

The rest is a maze of technical rules on keeping score and achieving victory over the opposing team. If, for example, you answered five questions correctly in a twenty-question round, you "quizzed out" and got to sit there on your chair in a retired glow as your less-worthy opponents, now relieved of your dominance, had a chance to score a few points of their own.

I did this from seventh grade all the way through my junior year in high school. Vast amounts of the King James went into my head and out of my mouth. Our team went to national finals where the pressure was intense. We never won at nationals, but we made a respectable showing. The winning team was rumored to get a free trip to Hawaii. This propelled me through many a dark valley in Quizland. I later found out that the trip was actually a missions trip, not a lie-on-the-beach sort of Hawaii experience. This softened the blow of never actually winning.

Now it may seem strange to encourage this combination of Bible memory and speech in a sort of competitive brew. But I was being prepared, in ways I didn't realize, to be comfortable on my feet with an internal grasp of God's Word. The motives were not the best, to be sure. But how else do you get teens to memorize that much Scripture? In the sort of mysterious way that God redeems all things, He was developing in me a sort of oral orientation toward Scripture—an ability to think on my feet and speak extemporaneously.

Think about how God has prepared you to preach. What were

your early impulses? What examples of preaching influenced you? How did God use circumstances and people in your call to preach? Perhaps you've never really identified the ways that God was working through your past. But I think there's something empowering about seeing God's hand in the story of our lives. God has called you to use your mouth for his glory. Moses and God had an argument about that when Moses was called (Exodus 3–4). The last thing Moses wanted to do was speak. He had a great fear of it. But over the course of his life the Lord did a great work. By the end of his life he made a grand address to the nation as they prepared to enter the land without him. He was eloquent. He was passionate. When you read the words, at the end of Deuteronomy, you wish you could hear it. And you remember the earlier argument and Moses' protest about being a lousy speaker. How gracious God is.

Decades after I finished Bible quizzing, I found out that all that verbal sparring, while odd by today's standards, would have been more commonplace in a much earlier age—an age when the spoken word was cultivated and honored, and education was driven toward creating orators who could speak well, more than scribes who could write well.

Beginning the Trip Backward

This capacity for what we're calling "orality," while still commonplace in the African American church,[1] has been increasingly lost in the world of mainstream preaching since the advent of the printing press. What I didn't realize as I was growing

---

1   I have found immediate consonance with black preachers when discussing oral homiletics. Though their impulses are not typically grounded in classical rhetoric (at least not the more published exponents), the oral sensorium is unmistakable. For the black preaching perspective, see Henry H. Mitchell's *Celebration and Experience in Preaching*, rev. ed. (Nashville: Abingdon, 2010); James Henry Harris's *The Word Made Plain: The Power and Promise of Preaching* (Minneapolis: Augsburg, 2004); or Cleophus J. LaRue's *The Heart of Black Preaching* (Louisville: Westminster John Knox, 2000).

up and beginning my life as a preacher was that the further we go back in church history, the more we find an oral orientation to preaching. In fact, the church was birthed in the golden age of oratory.

While we have steadily advanced in science and technology, our standards for good speaking have been on a steady decline. The apostles spoke and later wrote in an orally driven culture much different than our own. I believe, if we could somehow bring them forward in time, they would preach circles around us. They might marvel at our cell phones, but we would marvel at the way they prayed and preached out of deep internal resources. As C. S. Lewis cautioned, we cannot indulge in the kind of "chronological snobbery" that assumes we're always better than those before us.

In the last three hundred years we can trace a move away from oral roots toward an increasingly literary structuring of the sermon. That is, it began to be something literary in its very essence. In many ways the sermon has become detached from the character of the speaker and externalized into text. The printed outline and/or manuscript have come to define the sermon, supplemented in the last decade by screen-based presentations that project the sermon into something enormous—something much larger in the room than the preacher. All this is very modern.

But times are changing. A debate currently rages about how to connect with a postmodern generation. Perhaps if we look back to premodern times, we can find help connecting with today's evolving audience. After all, postmoderns and premoderns share many of the same viewpoints on communication.

In chapter 6 we'll see how Walter Ong reanimates this ancient world of Greco-Roman rhetoric. Walter Ong was not merely a contemporary scholar in orality, but also a classics scholar.[2] Clearly Ong knew where to go to find what has been neglected. But

---

2   In the 566-page *An Ong Reader: Challenges for Further Inquiry*, ed. Thomas J. Farrell and Paul A. Soukoup (Cresskill, NJ: Hampton, 2002), Ong cites Aristotle thirty-four times, Cicero seventeen times, Plato twenty-four times, Homer twenty-four times, and Quintilian fourteen times.

before we dig deeply into his work, let's first hear from the ancient world itself. Pontius Pilate's keen question to Jesus provides a bridge between classical rhetorical theory and our New Testament.

Pontius Pilate Weighs In

"What is truth?" Besides being a hotly contested question today, it is also Pilate's irritated reply to Jesus' claim about testifying to the truth (John 18:38). At first glance it seems to be simply the nervous maneuvering of a scared tyrant. But perhaps there is more to his conversation-ending question. Pilate was a well-educated Roman procurator grounded in the grammar and rhetoric of both classic Greece and Hellenized Rome.[3] Just a generation before him the politician and orator Cicero had demonstrated and documented the training in rhetoric that Pilate had no doubt studied back in Rome.

Pilate, then, would have had more than just cursory knowledge of classic philosophy and rhetoric. When he asked, "What is truth?" he wasn't just stalling. He was opening the can of worms that had been brewing for centuries in the ancient world. On the one side he was schooled regarding Plato's conception of the Philosopher, who loves the truth, and only the truth, despising all efforts to massage or exploit it for personal gain. On the other hand he knew the arguments of Plato's detractors, the Sophists, who questioned whether there is such a universal truth. The Sophists recognized that "truth" is articulated from a particular point of view, and those with varying points of view both claim to have truth on their side.[4] For the Sophist it was pointless to seek universal truth since all truth is situational and based in perception rather than reality. These are the same issues we wrestle with today.

So when Jesus testifies to "the Truth," Pilate knows his escape. Adopting a sophistic outlook, he reasons his way out as if to say: "Is the truth really so simple, Jesus? Is there only one truth? Would

---

3   Richard Leo Enos, *Roman Rhetoric: Revolution and the Greek Influence* (Prospect Heights, IL: Waveland, 1995), 69.

4   Plato's attacks on sophism can be easily referenced in the Gorgias dialogues. See Plato, *Gorgias* (New York: Classic Books America, 2009).

not your accusers also have their 'truth'? Doesn't truth depend on where one stands at any given moment? You quiz me as if there exists some obvious truth when in actuality, the world is a lot messier than that."

His tactic is to paint Jesus as simplistic and stuck in Plato's bygone era. "Any educated man knows," he might have told himself, "that an appeal to universal truth is impossible, delusional, and dangerous. No wonder he's gotten himself into trouble. This is how you get yourself killed. You try to prove something authoritatively to people who are just as authoritative as you are. I cannot help a man who will not help himself."

Pilate, often portrayed as flimsily paranoid, rarely gets credit for thinking on a philosophical level. We have a truncated version of him pulled from the Easter pageants, but uninformed by any broader context. So Pilate becomes a caricature of himself, and we lose the sense of what was really going on in that moment. His question to Jesus is a timeless one, bridging the issues of the ancient world with the church today in our postmodern culture. But to catch its relevance, we must have some sense of what the world was arguing about in the first century. Then we can see that some things never change and our so-called new issues are really quite old.

On the other hand, study of the ancient world also reveals some differences in how ideas were communicated. While reading and writing were certainly not rare skills in the first century AD, their purpose was fundamentally different. Communication was primarily oral with literacy serving in a backup role. To a large degree those tables have turned. We now think of generating sermons in literacy and then converting them to some form of orality on Sunday. So if we unreflectively read contemporary practice back onto ancient times, we miss the dynamic ways orality worked in the ancient world and how the Word originally was spoken.

Why Quintilian Matters

Marcus Fabius Quintilianus was born a Roman citizen in Spain in the first century AD. At the time he was born in roughly AD

40, the apostle Paul was preparing, with Barnabas, to take his first missionary journey on behalf of the burgeoning church headquartered in Antioch. Although we know little of his upbringing, we do know he was called from Spain to Rome in AD 68 by the Emperor Galba to establish a school of rhetoric. Interestingly, Paul was also called to Rome in AD 68, albeit as a condemned prisoner instead of a professor, and he was likely in Spain in that same decade. The two could feasibly have met. In another ironic twist, both Paul (Acts 25–26) and Quintilian (*Institutio oratoria* 4.2.19) pled cases before the Jewish queen Bernice. Quintilian, however, lived to around AD 100 or perhaps 118 (well past Paul who died shortly after his arrival in Rome), and was writing his *Institutes of Oratory*[5] in AD 90–95, just about the time the apostle John was finishing his Gospel.

This contextualization of his life places his work squarely in the time the church was just getting on its feet. Think about what that means. The ways he describes preaching and teaching were the ways it was being done in the book of Acts. When Paul or Peter spoke or later wrote, they spoke and wrote to audiences who operated according to these classic standards. The oral world of Cicero and Quintilian is the oral world of the New Testament. So the best clues we have about how the church communicated are found by digging into how communication actually worked at that time. This helps us see the early church through its own lens, not through our own. The closer we look, the more we see how the church in that world communicated differently than it does today.

Though he never mentions Christianity explicitly, his orientation to life, learning, and communication reflects the soil in which the church grew, spread, suffered, and matured.[6] Quintilian spent

---

5   Quintilian, *Institutes of Oratory*, ed. Lee Honeycutt, trans. John Selby Watson (1856; repr., Ames: Iowa State University, 2006), http://rhetoric .eserver.org/quintilian/. All subsequent citations refer to this hypertextual reprint edition, and the Latin title *Institutio oratoria* is used in parenthetical citations.

6   Scholars such as F. H. Colson and James R. Edwards have discerned similarities between chapter 1 of the *Institutes of Oratory* and the Gospel

the majority of his life teaching eloquence and arguing cases in Rome before retiring to document his approach in his only surviving work, *Institutes of Oratory*, which he composed when he was in his fifties.[7] Arguably the most influential educational theorist in Western civilization, he might be called the father of the liberal arts model, eventually adopted by most Christian schools.[8]

By the time of Quintilian, the Roman Republic (where laws were debated democratically) was a distant memory replaced by the iron fist of the Roman Empire. No longer were legislative issues debated in the public square. Yet the courts were still open and still demanded competent lawyers. Ceremonial speeches still played a role in reinforcing community values. While we're familiar with the image of Paul preaching in the open air in Athens, we need to remember that Christians weren't the only ones speaking in public. Speaking was going on all around them in highly sophisticated and carefully structured ways. While chapters 8 and 9 of this book apply some of Quintilian's rhetorical theory to preaching, at this stage one idea is central: *vir bonus*.

---

of Mark, suggesting that Quintilian was familiar with early Christian metaphors via his discourse with the Christian parents of two of his students. See F. H. Colson, "Quintilian, the Gospels and Christianity," *Classical Review* 39, nos. 7–8 (1925): 166–70; James R. Edwards, *The Gospel according to Mark* (Grand Rapids: Eerdmans, 2002), 8.

7   Quintilian's life was difficult, surviving the loss of a very young wife and losing two sons while they were still young boys. These losses are mentioned explicitly in his works, demonstrating the freedom felt by ancients to blend personal life and scholarship.

8   Jeffry Davis notes his influence and contributions made: "Given Quintilian's part in the establishment and promotion of the liberal arts tradition, his probable friendship with Christians of his day, and historical influence upon Christian scholars and teachers—notwithstanding his pedagogical contributions to the formation of virtuous students—proponents of Christian liberal arts have a clear and natural rationale for appropriating Quintilian's ideas." Jeffry C. Davis, "The Virtue of Liberal Arts: Quintilian and Character Education," *Journal of Interdisciplinary Studies* 19, nos. 1/2 (2007): 78.

Vir Bonus

The Latin term *vir bonus*, meaning a man of virtuous character, is perhaps the feature for which Quintilian is best known. For Quintilian, there is no separation of speech and speaker. Who a person is irrepressibly leaks into what is said.[9] "We are to form, then, the perfect orator, who cannot exist unless as a good man, and we require in him, therefore, not only consummate ability in speaking, but every excellence of mind" (*Institutio oratoria*, preface, 9).

For Quintilian, an orator draws deeply upon something as he speaks. It is not the external brute facts of a given case or matter, but the personal grasp a speaker has upon the situation as informed by moral character. The well from which he draws is internal and personal. "I am convinced that no one can be an orator who is not a good man, and even if anyone could, I should be unwilling that he should be" (1.2.3). An unprincipled preacher simply cannot draw deeply from internal resources so as to react to the moment in a grounded way. If the preacher is passing along secondhand truth, the essential connections between mind and mouth are missing.

This metaphor of deep resources comes straight from Quintilian's own pen: "No man will ever be thoroughly accomplished in eloquence who has not gained a deep insight into the impulses of

---

9   One cannot help but think of the consonance Quintilian shares with the apostle James' teaching on the power of the tongue: "The tongue is a small part of the body, and yet it boasts of great things. See how great a forest is set aflame by such a small fire! And the tongue is a fire, the very world of iniquity; the tongue is set among our members as that which defiles the entire body, and sets on fire the course of our life, and is set on fire by hell. For every species of beasts and birds, of reptiles and creatures of the sea, is tamed and has been tamed by the human race. But no one can tame the tongue; it is a restless evil and full of deadly poison. With it we bless our Lord and Father, and with it we curse men, who have been made in the likeness of God; from the same mouth come both blessing and cursing. My brethren, these things ought not to be this way. Does a fountain send out from the same opening both fresh and bitter water? Can a fig tree, my brethren, produce olives, or a vine produce figs? Nor can salt water produce fresh. Who among you is wise and understanding? Let him show by his good behavior his deeds in the gentleness of wisdom" (James 3:5–13).

human nature and formed his moral character on the precepts of others and on his own reflection" (12.2.4).[10] Note the things he has in mind as requirements: (1) deep insight into the motivations of human nature, (2) moral character formed by listening to others, and (3) personal reflection.

He is responding to the prevailing idea, in his day and ours, that to know a lot about a topic is enough. He is saying that cognitive understanding is not enough, even if we know it inside out. Knowledge is not enough. Or as Paul would say it, "Knowledge makes arrogant, but love edifies" (1 Cor. 8:1). Quintilian was concerned about the moral character that is forged in deep reflection. Deep reflection about what? About why people do what they do. Theologically, we call this anthropology. What drives people to act as they do? We are not prepared to speak unless we have a deep understanding of human motivation. This is wisdom as opposed to simple knowledge.

It is important to note the inherent value[11] Quintilian placed on moral character.[12] A truly decent person does not gain that decency to become a better speaker. What he aims for instead is the impractical pursuit of virtue. This reflective morality has to be acquired as an end in itself.[13] It's good enough just to be virtuous

---

10 Here again, "Also, in many passages both of his books and of his letters, Cicero remarks that the power of eloquence is to be derived from the deepest sources of wisdom, and that accordingly the same persons were for a considerable time the teachers at once of eloquence and of morality" (*Institutio oratoria* 12.2.6).

11 Quintilian left no doubt about this: "Nor is eloquence ever sought by us, because it is the most honorable and noble of attainments or for its own sake. . . . I would not wish to have even for a reader of this work a man who would compute what returns his studies will bring him" (1.12.16).

12 This understanding of the *vir bonus* is taken directly from a close read of Quintilian and not from an abstract understanding of "the good" from exterior sources (such as Ernest Brandenburg's meandering attempt to define it from disconnected sociological analysis in "Quintilian and the Good Orator," *Quarterly Journal of Speech* 34, no. 1 [1948]: 23–39).

13 Quintilian summarized this as follows: "With this character of it, the definition that oratory is the science of speaking well agrees excellently, for it embraces all the virtues of oratory at once and includes also the

even if we can't see how it will help our preaching. When this kind of character fuels the speech, the process is both complete and beautiful.

So here we have a pagan scholar who laid out for us something very profound—something with application to preaching. He said any attempt to prioritize preaching over character is not only wrong, it simply won't work. He can't stand dividing the world up into people who love truth (philosophers) and people who speak it (preachers). There is only the good man whose essential goodness leaks out in words.

Knowledge versus Wisdom

As we've acknowledged before, it's possible to preach more from knowledge than from wisdom. It's just impossible to do it without a creeping sense of distance between ourselves and our audience. A secondhand sermon, full of technically true ideals but devoid of personal reflection, can sound pretty good. People might even leave thinking it was pretty good. They might even admire a certain turn of the phrase or breadth of understanding or comic appeal. But it won't create connection and it won't inspire action. I've preached sermons where I was funny, even entertaining and very fluent. But my heart was missing. I've covered my lack of heart with humor and stories that are fun to tell. A preacher without deep reflection can hide even in the midst of a passionate delivery. So we have to be mindful that our words and tone demonstrate the deep reflection to which Quintilian refers.

As preachers, we ourselves are the undeniable limitation on whatever we might want to preach. We cannot separate character from preaching. The person who wants to preach well must not start with homiletics. We must pursue those "deep resources" that Quintilian keeps referring to. We must start with truth for truth's sake.

This is a challenge for preachers who must come up with a new

---

character of the true orator, as he cannot speak well unless he be a good man" (*Institutio oratoria* 2.15.34).

message fifty-two weeks a year. We find ourselves on a relentless search for material. Everything we read is potential sermon fodder. Every interaction is a potential sermon illustration. Something frustrating happens and we find ourselves quickly inserting it into the week's sermon outline. We even think to ourselves, "There now. That wasn't so bad. At least I got some use out of that irritation." Everything becomes appropriated for the sermon. Every movie is vying for mention. And here's where it gets dangerous: Scripture itself becomes mere fodder for sermon. This may seem inevitable at first. Of course the text is fodder for sermon. The sermon is based in the text. It could be no other way, right?

While the Scripture text and the sermon are inseparable, we must be careful not to use our study of Scripture to audition it for the next sermon. As preachers we need to keep a respect for Scripture as it is by itself, not merely as a tool for our profession. We must read it for its message and marinate our lives in it without jumping ahead and thinking, "This will preach."

This isn't limited to our use of Scripture. Other things can be improperly used. Sometimes, when we're in the middle of a conversation, my wife will say, "It sounds like you're teaching." I have this urge to turn everything into a lesson. It's almost as if I think I can't understand a thing unless I'm explaining it to someone else—that I learn by telling. But my so-called lesson becomes a departure from the personal conversation. It represents me leaving the shared moment and heading off toward my own private goal. It can make people feel used—and no wonder. They can easily be used, as can everything around me.

In contrast is Quintilian's *vir bonus*. As we heard from Augustine, this is the priority of being over telling. Anyone can tell. Telling is relatively easy. Telling can become, for the preacher, a quicker, more reliable substitute for being. Being requires me to operate independently of an audience. There is no reward in being like there is in telling. This is why Jesus removes the audience from all the acts of righteousness in the Sermon on the Mount. We are to pray in private, fast in private, and give secretly. It is what you do

when no one sees that is the test. Take the audience away and see
what is left. For many of us, perhaps not a lot. Have we found too
much significance in the telling? Are we babies in being? Can we
sit quietly with a text without thinking, "Have I got plans for you.
You and I are going to do great things together"?

Working On Our Preaching Without Working On Our Preaching

The implication here is that the preacher needs to have an
identity before God and people that is deeper than the preaching
role. We need to become lovers of God first. Lovers of people
second. Communicators only as the overflow and by-product of
those two things. Being a good preacher means prioritizing habits
that have no direct bearing on this week's tasks. We might choose
to start walking in the morning. We walk for the inherent value
of walking, not to accomplish anything measurable. We may not
see any connection between our choice to walk, and the rest of the
things that need to be done in a given week. But that's okay. Not
everything is instrumental or efficient. Sometimes I intentionally
take a longer, more scenic, route between two points for the sheer
luxury of being inefficient. Will the walking help us accomplish
more? Perhaps. Perhaps not. But it's the wrong question. Here's
the irony. Character builds sermons. But we don't seek character so
we can build a sermon.

This is why, to really preach better, we can't fixate simply on
preaching. There are other more weighty issues in play, things we
must look in the eye. We must face our struggling marriages, our
poor work ethic, our desperate lack of compassion, our hiding
and blaming. A dishonest, angry, or negligent preacher will never
produce a grounded sermon no matter how many commentaries
are consulted. We cannot escape ourselves, and until we face
ourselves our preaching cannot help but suffer.

All these things, the central issues of our lives, are where the
gospel meets us. It's the reason we ever wanted to preach in the
first place. They are prior to and under and then entangled in

our sermons. But when we commit to being honest and deeply devoted men and women, God has more to work with in the planning and preaching of a sermon. This is the essence of Quintilian's *vir bonus* as applied to preaching.

What It Looks Like

When preachers are concerned with character before sermon, they can no longer do business as usual. It's not enough to just hunt for other people's good ideas and compile them in a tasteful way. The preacher knows the sermon must come at some personal cost, that it's impossible to separate sermon and life. Illustrations are current and personal, not recycled out of distant times and places. The preacher is more than just a set of vocal chords reciting truisms. There is an embodiment of truth going on, where the preacher is actually animated and energized by internal realities.

Here's a test. Imagine a pretty good speaker who's not even a believer. Now suppose this person has solid communication skills: a good mind and a fluent vocabulary. Could this person, with a little practice, deliver your sermon as well as you? If so, there is not a lot of internal resource driving your sermon. It is information passed along. It lives outside of you. It is theoretically true, but not personally true.

In contrast, a sermon that is grounded in a personal experience of faith would be hard for someone else to emulate. They might see a phrase on your outline like "admitting guilt." They would understand, in principle, the concept of a guilty person who pleads guilty. But if they're not familiar with the personal phenomena of the weight of guilt and the relief of grace, their description will sound technical and academic. When we try to explain theological terms without personal grounding we might sound technically competent, but experientially we'll come across as flat.

The ancient orators had something else in mind. They had a kind of message that couldn't be just cut and pasted—something that couldn't be faked, that required the full heart and character and mind of the speaker. It is like something flowing organically out of a decent life. Quintilian called these "the essential connections."

Curiosity about Many Things

Though moral character is the foundation of Quintilian's theory, he also advocates three additional practices to build oral competence. The first of these is to foster a curiosity about many things. For a preacher, this requires interest in many subjects, not just those applicable to this week or next week's sermon.[14] We all have interests outside the realm of formal theology.[15] Those interests are not unspiritual. The ancients thought a variety of experience was necessary to stretch both mind and soul.[16]

Becoming deeper people has something to do with things as diverse as astronomy, cooking, the economy, and Ping-Pong. We have some sense of the interrelatedness of all things in our

---

14 About such curiosity Quintilian says, "Mute insects, too, compose the exquisite flavor of honey, inimitable by human reason, of various sorts of flowers and juices. Shall we wonder that eloquence, nothing more excellent than which the providence of the gods has given to men, requires the aid of many arts, which, even though they may not appear or put themselves forward in the course of a speech, yet contribute to it a secret power and are silently felt? 'People have been eloquent,' some one may say, 'without these arts'; but I want a perfect orator" (1.10.7–8).

15 Quintilian provides the basis for the Western liberal arts education when he advocates devotion to subjects as impractical as music (1.10.22) and geometry (1.10.34). Walter Ong traces this utilitarian role for rhetoric to the sixteenth-century attacks of Peter Ramus on all classical rhetoric including, most notably, Quintilian. "Quintilian's is a holistic idea, of the sort that lay at the heart of the Renaissance revival of rhetoric where the revival was most powerful. Rhetoric was of a piece with human existence, moral, civil, and eloquent: it called for human interaction at its peak. For Ramus, rhetoric was rather simply the art of verbal style and delivery." Walter J. Ong, review of *Arguments in Rhetoric against Quintilian: Translation and Text of Peter Ramus's* Rhetoricae Distinctiones in Quintilianum *(1549)*, by Peter Ramus, trans. Carole Newlands, *Quarterly Journal of Speech* 72, no. 2 (1987): 242.

16 Quintilian makes no apologies for the growing pains such varied learning entails: "If I seem to my reader to require a great deal, let him consider that it is an orator that is to be educated. . . . There is need of constant study, the most excellent teachers, and a variety of mental exercises" (*Institutio oratoria* 1.1.10).

"Father's world" as the old hymn called it. We are curious about the world not merely to appropriate it for a sermon, but to grow in our worship and love of God.

This curiosity transforms doctrine from cold statements of fact to living and dynamic descriptions of how the world around us actually works. A term like "redemption" must move from its dictionary definition toward an experiential sense of what it means to be in a process of lifelong change. We must grow in our ability to describe that process without scratching our heads and thinking, "Wait a minute, don't tell me. I know this." We spot redemption in everyday life when a daughter is healed, a lost dog is found, or a light comes on in a dark room. Redemption becomes that close to us. Close enough that it can leak into any conversation or sermon without even necessarily being planned. This is what the ancients meant when they said we need to know a little bit about everything to be ready to speak.

Imitation through Reading and Writing

As a second helpful practice, Quintilian advocates following the example of good speakers and authors through constant reading and writing. It's not just reading, but reading out loud that helps the most.[17] This is closer to an oral interpretation of the literature. Reading out loud not only focuses the student on the content at hand, but also toward its oral expression, inflection, and pace. Silent reading misses the whole point if we expect such reading to nurture fluent use of language. But reading good literature out loud, slowly but steadily, builds our abilities to frame language naturally and fluently.

Closely allied with reading is the discipline of writing.[18] But

---

17 Quintilian elaborates as follows: "Reading remains to be considered. Only practice can teach a boy to know when to take breath, where to divide a verse, where the sense is concluded, where it begins, when the voice is to be raised or lowered, what is to be uttered with any particular inflection of sound, or what is to be pronounced with greater slowness or rapidity, with greater animation or gentleness than other passages" (1.8.1).

18 With regard to writing Quintilian says, "We must write, therefore, as

this is not the writing of the sermon itself. This is writing just to express an idea well—writing a letter, an email, or a blog. It is writing that forms the capacity for natural-sounding speech. As with many arts, competence in fundamentals must be internally mastered before we can safely leave them behind. We learn the rules so that we can change the rules. This competence in reading and writing becomes a sort of imitation whereby our minds are indelibly imprinted with speech patterns. This is good and healthy imitation.[19]

This imitation should not be confused with modern notions of plagiarism. It is not exact content or specific expressions that we imitate, but the unique ways in which an author builds with language. Surely you've found yourself, after reading a favorite author for a long time, subconsciously mimicking the author's way of communicating. This is a good thing. Reading good writing builds overall verbal agility, though in a very slow and indirect manner. I remember once reading Jon Krakauer's *Into Thin Air* on vacation. I picked up the book in the afternoon and couldn't put it down until the wee hours. It was just exhilarating to sit that long with a master of prose. Do I expect that it helped me as a preacher? Not in any measurable way. But that's not why I did it.

---

carefully and as much as we can, for as the ground, by being dug to a great depth, becomes more fitted for fructifying and nourishing seeds, so improvement of the mind, acquired from more than mere superficial cultivation, pours forth the fruits of study in richer abundance and retains them with greater fidelity. For without this precaution, the very faculty of speaking extempore will but furnish us with empty loquacity and words born on the lips. In writing are the roots, in writing are the foundations of eloquence" (10.3.2–3).

19   Quintilian affirms the learning value of imitating the best of what has worked well for others: "From these authors and others worthy to be read, a stock of words, a variety of figures, and the art of composition must be acquired. Our minds must be directed to the imitation of all their excellences, for it cannot be doubted that a great portion of art consists in imitation, since, though to invent was first in order of time and holds the first place in merit, it is of advantage to copy what has been invented with success" (10.2.1).

The ancients maintained that if you do the right kinds of things, they will help you as a preacher. But you must not do those things to become a better preacher.

To apply this to the preacher's life we might say that journaling, while not specifically related to any sermon, is one way to build verbal confidence. We need to remember that ancient oratory assumes an extemporaneous delivery. In future chapters we'll explain more specifically what that means. For right now, think of it as a kind of speaking that requires us to trust our brains to be able to finish the sentence our mouth just started. We have a plan, a map as we'll later call it, but our actual words are coming out of our mouths as the moment dictates. This is the risky territory we spoke of earlier. But it becomes less risky and more natural as we use writing to improve our overall verbal competence and confidence.

Building Verbal Fluency

Quintilian's final practice is drawn from the ancient school environment in which emerging verbal skills were honed and refined through casual debate. This involved not only audible reading by students, but also the beginnings of an audience to whom such reading is directed.[20] There was a social sense to this kind of dialogue. It was best formed among peers and was not harmed by a mild sense of point and counterpoint.[21]

Quintilian wanted his students to have as much practice on their feet as possible.[22] The entire effort needed social interaction as the

---

20   Quintilian suggests the following: "But as soon as it shall be proper for him to read orations and when he shall be able to perceive their beauties, then, I would say, let some attentive and skillful tutor attend him who may not only form his style by reading, but oblige him to learn select portions of speeches by heart and to deliver them standing, with a loud voice, and exactly as he will have to plead so that he may consequently exercise by pronunciation both his voice and memory" (*Institutio oratoria* 1.11.14).

21   Quintilian says, "It is of advantage, therefore, for a boy to have schoolfellows whom he may first imitate and afterwards try to surpass. Thus will he gradually conceive hope of higher excellence" (*Institutio oratoria* 1.2.29).

22   This verbal sparring can include declamations, narrations, refutations,

soil for germinating speech. His laboratory of oratory was necessarily public and could not be conducted in privacy.[23] Private preparation gave a false sense of competence and readiness, but the speaker trained in public, even competitive, environments naturally developed oral confidence.[24]

If I go back to those old days of Bible quizzing, that's exactly what was happening and I didn't even realize it. All the memorization, all the time standing in front of the dreaded microphone while the judges calculated, all the mild competiveness with all the ribbons and ambition thrown in—those were all early ways of building verbal confidence.

Today I get some of that kind of interplay at a lunch table with other pastors and teachers. In that give-and-take of ideas and observations, I find my own thinking both challenged and clarified. Even family discussions at dinner or small group Bible studies are part of this process.

As I write this chapter, I have to write and rewrite. I have to hone my words to carry my ideas. But as I write, I become more

---

confirmations, praise of good characters, censure of evil, commonplaces, theses, comparisons, fictitious cases (as in *Institutio oratoria* 2.4), and also imitation of actual proceedings (2.10.12). Verbal sparring turns out to be the best predictor of success as a student. "I will venture to say that this sort of diligent exercise will contribute more to the improvement of students than all the treatises of all the rhetoricians that ever wrote" (2.5.14).

23 Quintilian explains why practicing one's oratory in private is inadequate as follows: "First of all, let him who is to be an orator and who must live amidst the greatest publicity and in the full daylight of public affairs, accustom himself, from his boyhood, not to be abashed at the sight of men, nor pine in a solitary and, as it were, recluse way of life. . . . Besides, when his acquirements are to be displayed in public, he is blinded at the light of the sun and stumbles at every new object, as having learned in solitude that which is to be done in public" (*Institutio oratoria* 1.2.18–19).

24 Michael Mendelson documents Quintilian's use of *controversia* as a pedagogical technique that needs revival in today's schools. Calling it "inherently dialogical," Mendelson aspires to a role for rhetoric that is truly epistemic in its formation of beliefs in the midst of competing truth claims. Michael Mendelson, "Quintilian and the Pedagogy of Argument," *Argumentation* 15, no. 3 (2001): 277–94.

clear in my own thinking. When I speak on this topic, I will be aided greatly by this exercise in writing. Not because I'll have a manuscript to read from, but because I will have wrestled with things until they have moved from external concepts to internal realities. And then all kinds of options open up in whatever setting I find myself. Quintilian has shown us that literacy and orality are not enemies. Though we must be orally equipped to speak from internally grounded reservoirs, those same reservoirs are filled by all sorts of things that we learn through reading and writing, listening and speaking.

The goal is to become a well-rounded person, not to produce a well-crafted sermon. It's the person whose walking, cooking, reading, journaling, discussing, disagreeing, fishing, crying, observing, praying, waltzing, welding, and wishing supplies the words they say on Sunday. It takes a whole person to preach well. Not a technocrat, not a grandstander, not a private scholar in the study. It's a public life well lived, and a life that overflows toward others.

PART 2

DEVELOPING AN
ORALLY BASED
MODEL OF PREACHING

5

WHY GOD IS PARTIAL TO THE SPOKEN WORD

According to our way of thinking you would think the Lord would at least have put off being born until after the invention of printing, that until then there had been no fullness of time, and that he would have secured for himself a few high-speed presses.

Søren Kierkegaard, *Papers and Journals*

I was thirteen when I got my first adult Bible. The event was, in my tradition, a loosely configured Protestant bar mitzvah. Not that I hadn't owned a Bible before. On any given day you might see a half dozen scattered around the house and another couple still in the car since Sunday. As a kid I had any number of disposable Bibles: paperbacks, junior versions with pictures, tiny New Testaments and Gideon-distributed versions. But it wasn't until that birthday that I got my first leather-bound edition.

On "Bookish" Bibles

This new Bible was a navy blue *Scofield Reference Bible.* It was scaled down smartly to be a little more compact than the standard size Scofield. I liked that feature. It was beautiful. It was a booklover's book: silver-edged pages and a delicate silk ribbon. Its pages were stuck together with that beautiful old tendency of fine paper. The first time two pages were separated they had a slight resistance. You had to delicately coax them apart. Each page felt like a new revelation, like an envelope's unsealing. You got the sense that no one had ever viewed it before. I knew that in getting me this book, my parents were acknowledging that I was ready to do serious study. It was intended as a blessing, and that's how I took it. I wanted to live up to the blessing and take it seriously.

I knew that had something to do with annotations, and not the notes already supplied by the Scofield editors. We adorned our Bibles with lots of handwritten notes. When your Bible was full of notes, it meant you were a serious student. These were evidence of a personal acquaintance with something. I knew my parents' Bibles were full of such things, passed down from previous eras.

So I did what any Bible-respecting teen would do: I set about to copy every note, page by page, from my mother's Bible into mine. This job was made slightly easier by the fact that we had identical versions right down to the page numbers. I wanted everything in mine that she had in hers. I wanted to look like a serious student. I don't know how far I got, a couple hundred pages for sure. I remember being relieved when I would encounter multiple pages that had little to no annotations. But other parts showed a myriad of tiny words and hand-scrawled diagrams. This was a daunting effort and eventually I ran out of steam.

I never really used that Bible. Perhaps it was because I always saw it as a sort of unfinished project. Perhaps my penmanship, never my strongest asset, had trouble matching my mother's careful script. Perhaps it was because that Bible was too nice to use. Perhaps I was saving this book for something special. But the Bible I used and abused was more the disposable kind. With all that weekly Bible quizzing work, I needed a Bible I could toss around and shove into a backpack. My Scofield was too precious for that.

So what is the nature of this book we have come to both revere and casually regard? Clearly it comes to us full of text. But what kind of text? Some of it was written before it was ever spoken. And some of it was spoken before it was ever written. We might call the former "written writing" and the latter "oral writing" (which sounds like an oxymoron). Before we go any further down the road toward orality, we must get some scriptural input on this whole topic. What does Scripture say about its own very nature? If revelation is fundamentally text, how do we deal with the fact that most of the people of God, down through the ages, unlike me and my precious Scofield, didn't have a personal Bible of their own? It comes to us now as text. But does that mean that literacy is necessary to receive God's Word? Let's start with the role of revelation in the lives of believers before our time.

General Literacy in the Ancient World

One of the oddest things about Jesus, from a literary perspective, is that, as far we know, he didn't write anything (save perhaps that scrawling in the sand mentioned in John 8 when the woman was caught in adultery). From the perspective of literacy we might assume that he would have. After all, everything authoritative is written, right? But Jesus didn't carry a scroll around. He did read from a scroll when he went to the synagogue. But most of the time he spoke as an author. He authored words out loud; words that, some thirty years later, were finally captured in text. It is the text that makes his words repeatable and preservable. Regardless of denomination, contemporary church life is inextricably linked to Scripture. It is almost impossible to imagine a church setting today without the presence of the biblical text in liturgy, doctrine, and preaching.

Since the modern world is so saturated with print culture, this omnipresence of sacred text seems commonplace, even indispensable. Since 1611 the King James Version and later translations have staked a claim of prominence in every avenue of church life. Indeed in the sixteenth and seventeenth centuries the Bible took its place along with other books on the shelves of European parishes and personal households in a way unimaginable even a hundred years before when only the wealthiest could have acquired a personal manuscript.[1] This had an individualizing effect

---

1   Make no mistake. Early printed Bibles, though more commonly available after Gutenberg, were still not acquired on whimsy. M. H. Black likens the resulting change that occurred after Gutenberg, in the sense of sacrifice

on the reader who now "owned" the text in more ways than one.[2] It must have been strange in those days to see people carrying around the first portable Bible. It might be comparable to today's proliferation of mobile Bibles on phones and tablets. It's strange, at first, to see the Bible called up this way. But eventually it will become second nature, as it already is for many younger believers. Perhaps it won't be long before we stop thinking of the Bible as a paper book at all.

What followed, way back then, was a demystifying of sacred text that was the natural consequence of mass production.[3] Early books, hand-copied, were treated with a sense of awe. But that was changed in the seventeenth century with the birth of the portable book and the portable, personal Bible. But this was not until some sixteen centuries after Christ and some thirty-six centuries after Abraham. For approximately 90 percent of the history of God's people, there were no personal Bibles feasibly owned by commoners.[4]

---

involved with buying a Bible, to buying a car (in Europe) instead of buying a house. M. H. Black, "The Printed Bible," in *The Cambridge History of the Bible* (Cambridge: Cambridge University Press, 1963), 3:424.

2   McLuhan observes, "The portability of the book, like that of the easel-painting, added much to the new cult of individualism." Marshall McLuhan, *The Gutenberg Galaxy: The Making of Typograhic Man* (Toronto: University of Toronto Press, 1962), 206.

3   Quoting Febvre and Martin's *L'Apparition du Livre*, McLuhan describes a sort of secularization that occurred: "Moreover, thanks to printing and the multiplication of texts, the book ceased to seem to be a precious object to be consulted in a library: there was more and more need to be able to carry it about readily in order to refer to it or to read it anywhere at any time" (*Gutenberg Galaxy*, 207).

4   Distinguishing elite from commoner is essential when contemplating ancient literacy. Though it is not difficult to find widespread references to literacy among the ruling class in Greece from 700 BC onward, the literacy level among commoners is an entirely different question. For more on this, see William V. Harris, *Ancient Literacy* (Cambridge: Harvard University Press, 1989), 231. Harris finds theological literacy among commoners far from essential in the Late Republic and High Roman Empire: "It was not necessary for an ordinary Christian to read any text for himself, although

Obstacles to Biblical Literacy

Consider the obstacles to a medieval tanner who, curious about the Bible he heard recited on Sunday, wanted to have a look for himself.[5] First, there was the geographic obstacle. The tanner would have to travel to a point where a copy of the text was housed. The most likely location would have been the local parish or regional monastery. At least there he might be able to make an intelligent and humble inquiry. Assuming he was able to make the trip and was deemed important enough to secure the attention of the parish priest or monk, he would likely encounter another procedural obstacle. The priest would surely not hand over a rare and costly text to a tanner untrained in the careful handling of such delicacies. Handwritten manuscripts had to last for decades, if not longer, and could be maintained only with special attention and reverence. But suppose the priest was kind enough to grant at least a supervised visit. He would lead the tanner to the place of safekeeping and open the massive codex.[6]

There the tanner would encounter for the first time the sensory stimuli offered by the smell and texture of the written word. But he would also encounter a conceptual barrier, as his own illiteracy would render the scratchings on the page unintelligible. Yet suppose the priest was extraordinarily gracious and offered to regularly tutor the tanner to the point where he could, with expert coaching, begin to pronounce the syllables of the revered Vulgate. He would then face the language barrier since, while some of the

---

the real enthusiast might of course wish to do so" (221).

5   The choice of a medieval example is important here, as most scholars attest to a general decline of literacy in the Late Empire with the barbarian invasions (Harris, *Ancient Literacy*, 321; S. L. Greenslade, ed., "Epilogue," in *Cambridge History of the Bible*, 3:491). Literacy's low ebb seems to have been roughly between AD 500 and 1200.

6   Harris describes the Christian's peculiar preference for the codex over the scroll in late antiquity, perhaps because printing on both sides of the parchment was economical, and because Christians acquired an early propensity toward polemic citations, a task made infinitely easier with the codex over the scroll (*Ancient Literacy*, 295–96).

words had a familiar liturgical ring, they would have been largely incomprehensible to the tanner accustomed to Medieval French or Old English.

These obstacles kept the sacred text inaccessible for countless generations of Jews and Christians before the arrival of print, contemporary translations, and the push toward mass literacy. "In these circumstances," observed history professor William V. Harris, "it seems perfectly natural that nothing like mass literacy ever came into being in antiquity."[7] Most of the people of God, for most of sacred history, have had to get along in the faith without the benefit of a personal Bible or any sustained and systematic obligation to read it for themselves. Somehow common folk were converted, prayed, parented, served, evangelized, learned biblical content, and activated their faith in the world using only the oral/aural[8] reception of the Word of God that they heard articulated from the synagogue or parish lectern.[9]

This is not to say we should seek a return to a bygone era by abandoning personal copies of the Bible or personal Bible reading.[10] But it does say something about our modes of reception of the Word of God, and might bring into question whether the stockpiles of personal Bibles that surround us in ever-expanding versions and colors actually make us better Christians than our forefathers without such benefit. It says something about the

---

7   Ibid., 327.

8   These two words are, ironically, linked in both sound and meaning. Though spelled differently they're pronounced the same, the first meaning something spoken and the second something heard.

9   Harris explains why the oral/aural transmission of the Scriptures dominated in the early church: "For the ordinary Christian, though the authority of the written word was in the background, there was no need for personal reading. . . . The church's leaders recognized that if Christian writings were to have much effect on the masses, they would have to be transmitted orally. In the second century, the scriptures were normally heard" (Harris, *Ancient Literacy*, 305).

10   Walter Ong, champion of orality, himself pointed out the naïveté and futility of such a longing. Walter J. Ong, *Orality and Literacy: The Technologizing of the Word* (New York: Routledge, 2002), 171.

oral/aural power of the Word of God as experienced in shared community and the resulting obligations to the preacher. If congregations are actually designed to hear the Word of God, and if that is exactly how the vast majority of our spiritual ancestors carried on in the faith, how should preaching attempt to honor and accommodate that design? What does biblical history teach us about human capacity to hear the Word of God?

Orality and Literacy in Partnership throughout Scriptural Transmission

Since, historically speaking, we must admit that the Bible had to be received orally for centuries before it was textually common, could it be that the Bible itself is orally generated and designed— even in its present textual form—to be heard first? Perhaps we are conditioned to overlook orality in ancient texts because we are so accustomed to wearing the spectacles of literacy when we read.[11]

Scripture itself tells us about its very nature.[12] In the sections that follow, we will examine four periods of God's revelation to

---

11   Walter Ong describes how our immersion in literacy affects how we view Scripture: "The same disability has interfered with our understanding of the nature of the Bible with its massive oral underpinnings, and that of the nature of language itself." Walter J. Ong, *The Presence of the Word: Some Prolegomena for Cultural and Religious History* (New Haven, CT: Yale University Press, 1967), 21.

12   Susan Niditch has done an important work here uncovering the behind-the-scenes interplay between orality and literacy that erupt in the Old Testament Scriptures. See Susan Niditch, *Oral World and Written Word: Ancient Israelite Literature* (Louisville: Westminster John Knox, 1996). Central to her thesis is the idea that we have largely ignored the oral underpinnings of Scripture because of the assumptions fostered by largely literate presuppositions. Niditch documents not only the sound patterns embedded in sacred text, but also the mysterious and magical power granted to literacy by illiterates and how that respect contributes to a sense of textual authority bordering on veneration. Following the oral interpretive pattern, Bruce Shields unmasks oral patterns in Luke, Acts, and the Epistles. See Bruce E. Shields, *From the Housetops: Preaching in the Early Church and Today* (St. Louis: Chalice Press, 2000).

see the ways in which Scripture is oral as well as written. We will sample the period of Moses and the Law, the prophet Jeremiah with his scribal assistant Baruch, the teaching and practice of Jesus, and the epistles of Paul to discern how Scripture itself frames the delicate balance.

With a keen grasp of the obvious, we first observe that the Scriptures we seek to consult on these issues are themselves written. So perhaps the inquiry is hopelessly tilted toward literacy. But the present form of Scripture, though written, was often previously spoken.

Look, for instance, at one of the familiar New Testament passages about prophecy: "Know this first of all, that no prophecy of Scripture is a matter of one's own interpretation, for no prophecy was ever made by an act of human will, but men moved by the Holy Spirit spoke from God" (2 Peter 1:20–21). The text clearly states that when God inspired the prophets, they *spoke*. The verbs that describe prophetic action are very vocal, very oral.[13]

Yet most commentaries overlook this and refer perpetually to the prophets as mere writers of Scripture. This is reading back onto them an immersion in literacy that is simply inaccurate.[14] That some of the prophets, and many of the historians of the Bible

---

13   Louis Schökel notes the verbal and oral cues present in the writings of the prophets: "Another series of facts indicate that part of the biblical literature had a prehistory in which it existed in oral form. The basic task of the prophets was that of proclaiming the word, and we see this in the accounts they leave of their vocation and descriptions such as that of the 'evangelist' or herald of good news in Isaiah 40:9, who is bidden to 'cry out at the top of your voice.'" Louis Alonso Schökel, *The Inspired Word: Scripture in the Light of Language and Literature*, trans. Francis Martin (New York: Herder and Herder, 1965), 247.

14   Schökel points out how our literary culture today affects how we tend to engage the prophetic sections of Scripture: "In a culture in which writing is already prevalent and predominant, there is a danger that some authors will lose awareness and feeling for the primary reality of the spoken word. They think in terms of letters, rather than in terms of sound, and they imagine that others near them or far from them in time or distance think, or thought, as they do" (ibid., 242).

wrote, is indisputable. But that many of them used secretaries (as Jeremiah and Paul did explicitly) is also beyond dispute.[15] Even when the text says that Isaiah or Jeremiah wrote on a book or scroll (Isa. 30:8 or Jer. 30:2), it no more guarantees they actually handled the stylus than Solomon's building of the temple guarantees he wielded the stonemason's hammer himself.

So we can see and hear that the transmission of Scripture is a confusingly beautiful blend of oral and literate sources.[16] To avoid reading our literate selves back onto the original speakers and authors, we must come to hear and recognize the often overlooked oral roots in our textual versions.[17] We'll try to avoid this imbalance in our survey of the sacred text.

Moses and the Law (First Period)

In only the third sentence of Moses' law, we hear the creative power of the voice of God. "Then God said, 'Let there be light'; and there was light" (Gen. 1:3). It is God's voice that continues through each successive day of creation. There was sound even before there were human ears to hear it. It all starts with sound, not sight.[18] This is the power of the primordial Word of God. It

---

15 For a scholarly overview of the pervasive role of the secretary in first-century literacy and in Paul's letters specifically, see E. Randolph Richards, *The Secretary in the Letters of Paul*, WUNT II 42 (1988; Tübingen: J. C. B. Mohr [Paul Siebeck], 1991). Richards documents evidence of a secretary in virtually all of Paul's letters, and especially Romans (which he conceives to have been dictated live), Galatians, and 1 Corinthians (ibid., 172).

16 Niditch proposes four etiologies of the written text and admits there may be more: (1) oral performance dictated and copied, (2) oral narrative documented for the purpose of reoralization, (3) literary composition imitating an oral style, and (4) written sources for written compositions (*Oral World and Written Word*, 117–29).

17 Schökel recognizes this interplay even in his description of inspiration, which he classifies with three simultaneous orders: "inspiration in the order of knowledge—cognitive; inspiration in the order of speech—prophetic; inspiration in the order of writing—hagiographical" (*Inspired Word*, 239).

18 Calvin reasons as follows: "For because something begins to be manifested at a certain time, we ought not therefore to gather that it never existed

is sound rather than sight that first entered the universe. Sound creates the world of sight. God is a God who has sounded his creation, a priority that must not be shrugged off.[19]

God's voice begins all new revelation. We are so accustomed to seeing the Ten Commandments in text, that it is hard for us to remember they were not originally delivered via text, but by God's own voice as a direct encounter.[20] Before he ever carved them in stone, he spoke them audibly as the record in Exodus 20:1 clearly shows ("Then God spoke all these words, saying . . ."). The people, hearing God's voice, were understandably alarmed and begged Moses not to make them hear such a thing ever again. It is clear they would rather have had Moses engage Yahweh personally. The Lord concurred but not without a stern reminder: "Thus you shall say to the sons of Israel, 'You yourselves have seen that I have spoken to you from heaven'" (Exod. 20:22).

Moses was then called up to the mountain where God again spoke, expanding the original Ten Commandments into the full covenant. Moses returned and orally delivered this fuller sense of the Law to the people. After hearing it, the people announced their willingness to obey. It was only then that "Moses wrote down all the words of the LORD" (Exod. 24:4). But it is significant

---

before. Indeed, I conclude far otherwise: the Word had existed long before God said, 'Let there be light.'" John Calvin, *Institutes of the Christian Religion*, trans. Ford Lewis Battles, ed. John T. McNeill (Philadelphia: Westminster, 1960), 1.13.8.

19 Stephen Webb discusses how the theology of sound and hearing defines us in relation to God as his creatures: "Theologically construed, speaking is not a trait projected upon God by analogy to human experience. We do not speak first, and then think about God as speaking too. On the contrary, we can speak only because God created us to be hearers of God's Word." Stephen H. Webb, *The Divine Voice: Christian Proclamation and the Theology of Sound* (Grand Rapids: Brazos, 2004), 15.

20 Though both Moses and angels are often connected to the giving of the Law, Aquinas makes this unmediated nature of divine revelation clear and significant: "It seems that the Old Law was not given through the angels, but immediately by God. . . . But the Old Law is related to have been given by the Lord: for it is written (Exod. 20:1): 'And the Lord spoke . . . these words'" (*Summa Theologica* II-I, Q 98, A 3, arg. 1).

to note that their first two exposures to the Law were oral and spoken. The written only came afterward to preserve. Spanning chapters 24 to 31, God called Moses up to the mountain a third time and spoke yet another expansion of the Law. Every revelation of the law or instruction given to Moses was spoken first. At the end of this third disclosure, God made a move toward preservation of his Word: "When He had finished speaking with him upon Mount Sinai, He gave Moses the two tablets of the testimony, tablets of stone, written by the finger of God" (31:18).

There are only a few times in the entire Bible when we are told that God himself wrote. There is this occurrence, and the second round when God replaced the tablets that Moses shattered. Aside from God's Son writing in the sand as mentioned earlier, the only other instance is the mysterious hand that suddenly began writing on the wall at Belshazzar's feast in the book of Daniel. But even when God does write, it is usually preceded by the spoken word with text in a preservative role. This is consistent with the overall role of literacy in the ancient world in which writing was used primarily to document speech.

At the end of Exodus 32, Moses and God both refer to a book of God's: "'But now, if You will, forgive their sin—and if not, please blot me out from Your book which You have written!' The LORD said to Moses, 'Whoever has sinned against Me, I will blot him out of My book'" (vv. 32–33). Although the reference is cryptic, it seems that at least in a metaphorical sense, God was keeping some kind of record or archive of faithfulness of which he and Moses are both aware. The book serves a documentary, archiving role, not the focus of new thought or discourse or revelation. References to books and scrolls and annals are commonplace throughout the Old Testament, almost always placing literacy as the means for preserving information that should not be forgotten and might need to be authenticated. Written words have a sort of legal sense to them. So when a man wants to initiate a divorce, he must get it drawn up to garner the legal sense of permanence (Deuteronomy 24).

Consider the instance in Numbers 5:22–24 where a woman was

suspected of adultery. The priest was instructed to write the curses on a scroll, and then wash the ink of the words into water that the woman then had to drink. The ink carried the legal sense of the curse into the water and the water into the woman. This is reminiscent of similar events later in Israel's history when a prophet was told to eat a scroll, moving the words of the text from the exterior to the interior of the person (Ezek. 3:1). The text, or in this case the ink, had a binding, permanent, and official sense that contrasts sharply with the fleeting nature of oral speech which, while equally authoritative, is difficult to capture and hold.

In Deuteronomy 6:4–9, the famous Shema of Israel, we see an interesting blend of the oral and the written.

> Hear, O Israel! The LORD is our God, the LORD is one! You shall love the LORD your God with all your heart and with all your soul and with all your might. These words, which I am commanding you today, shall be on your heart. You shall teach them diligently to your sons and shall talk of them when you sit in your house and when you walk by the way and when you lie down and when you rise up. You shall bind them as a sign on your hand and they shall be as frontals on your forehead. You shall write them on the doorposts of your house and on your gates.

The initial call is from orality: "Hear," not "Read, O Israel!" It is the ear that receives revelation. From the ear it moves to a place "on your heart." This is an acceptance or interiorization of the Word. From the heart it goes back to the mouth as the commands are orally taught in the normal discourse of shared community life. Then the move is toward preservation as they become "tied" and "bound" with visual symbols and "written" on the doorposts and gates. Again revelation starts in orality and then is captured by literacy.[21]

---

21 This sort of progression is difficult to document from typical exegetical research methods. Aquinas and Augustine cite this passage voluminously, linked as it usually is, with Trinitarian controversy. But the entire point for most scholars is in the text that follows the familiar "Hear, O Israel!"

Another preservative role for literacy is in the training of kings. The Lord required that every king be literate enough to have firsthand acquaintance with the Law: "Now it shall come about when he sits on the throne of his kingdom, he shall write for himself a copy of this law on a scroll in the presence of the Levitical priests. It shall be with him and he shall read it all the days of his life, that he may learn to fear the LORD his God, by carefully observing all the words of this law and these statutes" (Deut. 17:18–19). The king here is reduced to scribe or copyist. He is not generating new information or discovering creative writing, but using the strengths of literacy to perpetuate already-given revelation and his personal connection to it.

At the end of Moses' life, as Deuteronomy comes to a close, documentation of the spoken word occurs everywhere. There is the sense, long before the book ends, that with Moses' death an era is passing. The spokesman of God will no longer be on the scene. There is a need to preserve, and literacy rises to the challenge. Moses, or his scribe, writes about his own writing and preservation of the Law. But since the bulk of the people are still not going to have their own copies of the Law, Moses requires the hearing and singing of the Law.

> Then Moses commanded them, saying, "At the end of every seven years, at the time of the year of remission of debts, at the Feast of Booths, when all Israel comes to appear before the LORD your God at the place which He will choose, you shall read this law in front of all Israel in their hearing. Assemble the people, the men and the women and children and the alien

---

The actual oral sense of the calling is not therefore pertinent and goes unnoted. Older commentators comfortable in orality do not typically call attention to oral/aural underpinnings possibly because it would seem to them little more than stating the obvious. Modern commentators ensconced in literacy tend to conflate oral and literate renditions of the Word of God into a generic sense of revelation. Commentators of all ages tend to focus on the content of the revelation rather than on its medium or the concomitant sensorium. In short, massive amounts of biblical orality go unnoticed.

who is in your town, so that they may hear and learn and fear the LORD your God, and be careful to observe all the words of this law. Their children, who have not known, will hear and learn to fear the LORD your God, as long as you live on the land which you are about to cross the Jordan to possess." (Deut. 31:10–13)

At least every seven years, during the sabbath year, the entire assembly was to hear the Law (Deut. 31:10–13). One might wonder if once every seven years was enough exposure since a person might only hear the Word at the most ten times their entire life, assuming the sabbatical year was faithfully observed.

But there were other ways that ancient cultures preserved on a widespread and oral level what was officially documented in writing. The same chapter has the Lord commanding the use of a communal and oral resource.

Now therefore, write this song for yourselves, and teach it to the sons of Israel; put it on their lips, so that this song may be a witness for Me against the sons of Israel. . . . Then it shall come about, when many evils and troubles have come upon them, that this song will testify before them as a witness (for it shall not be forgotten from the lips of their descendants); for I know their intent which they are developing today, before I have brought them into the land which I swore." So Moses wrote this song the same day, and taught it to the sons of Israel. (Deut. 31:19, 21–22)

Chapter 32 records the song that could be used to perpetuate, in shared memory, God's direct revelation. The song itself is disquieting, a prediction of unfaithfulness and punishment and defeat. It may not be pleasant to be asked to sing their own failures, but it is the kind of oral resource that gave the community strength when it had no widespread or predictable access to the written Law. Chapter 32 is a strong prescription in the communal medicine chest, but it is not the only one.

Chapter 33 is also an extended song, although with a more optimistic outlook.

> Indeed, He loves the people;
>> all Your holy ones are in Your hand,
>> and they followed in Your steps;
>> everyone receives of Your words.
> Moses charged us with a law,
>> a possession for the assembly of Jacob. (vv. 3–4)

Notice the Law is the "possession of the assembly." The notion of private ownership of the Law would have been foreign indeed. The song then celebrates some aspect of each tribe. About Levi he says:

> They shall teach Your ordinances to Jacob,
>> and Your law to Israel.
> They shall put incense before You,
>> and whole burnt offerings on Your altar. (v. 10)

This is the specified role of the Levites: maintaining the sacrificial system, and instructing the people in the Law. If we conceive of the task from the modern perspective of literacy, we think immediately of textual resources. But how would they teach such a vast illiterate throng? Certainly the oral resources of poetry and song would have been helpful. Besides the entire songbook of Psalms, songs are scattered throughout the Old Testament, often recounting salvation history in memorable sequence.

During the postexilic revival under Ezra and Nehemiah, the Levitical teaching role is explicit, moving from text to recitation to oral commentary.

> The Levites . . . explained the law to the people while the people remained in their place. They read from the book, from the law of God, translating to give the sense so that they understood the reading. (Neh. 8:7–8)

Notice their role encompassed both oral and literate tasks: reading from the Law and also providing explanation and application along with translation. The auditory role of public reading is familiar and typical of how people experienced the Word of God. The explanatory role, though previously implied in Levitical responsibility, is listed here explicitly as part of the Levitical job description and is the closest approximation of modern preaching we get anywhere in the Old Testament. The Levites started with silent text, read it audibly, and then made application and comment to the congregation. From the divinely creative word, to the delivery of the Law, to its reception and application, the Pentateuch gives a consistent sequence: new revelation was spoken first, only later to be written down.

Jeremiah and Baruch (Second Period)

About one hundred years before the Babylonian exile, Jeremiah spoke to Judah during the waning days of the southern kingdom. An episode from chapter 36 gives us insight into the ways that orality and text worked in revelation and preaching. During the reign of King Jehoiakim, the kingdom continued its deterioration. While there had been a literacy-driven revival under Jehoiakim's father, Josiah, who found the long lost book of the law, Jehoiakim was a puppet king installed by Pharaoh Neco and had none of the heart of his father. Jeremiah was told by God to write down all the words God had spoken to the prophet for at least the last four years, probably more. Jeremiah secured a scribe named Baruch to take dictation and produce a written record. So the pattern from Moses continues: revelation starts in the spoken word, and then is recorded for documentation.

In this case, the specific purpose is the portability of God's Word. Jeremiah, either because of personal threat or a type of restraining order, was forbidden to approach the temple in Jerusalem. Yet with the miracle of literacy, his words, carried and reanimated by Baruch, could. Baruch followed the instructions and went to the temple to read to the assembly. It just so happened that Micaiah, grandson of the secretary who had found and read the law in the previous administration, overheard Baruch's public reading and reported it immediately to the palace officials. Micaiah was typical of the professional scribe, elevated above commoners and nobles alike by his proficiency in literacy.

They promptly summoned Baruch and requested a more private, yet still audible reading. Baruch complied and once again read them the text. Alarmed, they recognized either Jeremiah's content or style or both. Upon inquiry, Baruch identified Jeremiah as the source, which furthered the probe. Suspecting the king might take retaliatory action, they instructed Baruch to take Jeremiah and hide, and then informed the king of the presence of the scroll. The king then called for yet another reading of the confiscated scroll.

> Now the king was sitting in the winter house in the ninth month, with a fire burning in the brazier before him. When Jehudi had read three or four columns, the king cut it with a scribe's knife and threw it into the fire that was in the brazier, until all the scroll was consumed in the fire that was in the brazier. Yet the king and all his servants who heard all these words were not afraid, nor did they rend their garments. (Jer. 36:22–24)

What is supposed to be striking is the apparent carelessness with which Jehoiakim dismisses and then destroys the scroll. He is the entirely profane man who not only ignores the words of the Lord, but also proceeds to ceremoniously destroy them. But just when it seems he has successfully thwarted the plan of God, we are reminded that God has hidden his prophet and his scribe.

> Then the word of the LORD came to Jeremiah after the king had burned the scroll and the words which Baruch had written at the dictation of Jeremiah, saying, "Take again another scroll and write on it all the former words that were on the first scroll which Jehoiakim the king of Judah burned. . . ." Then Jeremiah took another scroll and gave it to Baruch the son of Neriah, the scribe, and he wrote on it at the dictation of Jeremiah all the words of the book which Jehoiakim king of

Judah had burned in the fire; and many similar words were added to them. (Jer. 36:27–28, 32)

Despite the king's irreverence and power, God's revelation could not be destroyed because it lived first in Jeremiah before it was ever exported to Baruch and the scroll.[22] Now the Lord could have as easily protected the scroll as he protected Jeremiah, but the priority of the prophet over the scroll seems to be the point. Revelation is generated orally and preserved in literacy. If the literacy were to be somehow destroyed, it is only a small effort for Jeremiah to restore it. In fact, the second scroll ends up longer and better than the first, a feature familiar to anyone who has lost a file and had to start from scratch rebuilding it.

So we see a very oral image of Jeremiah often overlooked in a literary mindset. He is a preacher more than he is a writer. In fact it is doubtful, given the explicit role of Baruch, that Jeremiah wrote very much at all. Consider his summary calling in 1:9: "Then the Lord stretched out His hand and touched my mouth, and the Lord said to me, 'Behold, I have put My words in your mouth.'" The divine call is clear along with its medium. God initiated prophets to speak first and foremost. "Thus saith the Lord" means enunciated sound, and prophets are God's tool to speak into his created order.

Yet since we only read about that calling to preach via text on a page, it is easy to confuse the two means for communication, and frame Jeremiah and his prophetic colleagues as authors first, bent faithfully in candlelight over a well-worn desk with stacks of parchments and papyri lying about. Now it seems likely that Jeremiah did write as his last ceremonial act. His instructions reveal his own understanding of the role of literacy: "So Jeremiah wrote in a single scroll all the calamity which would come

---

22 Niditch explains further: "The oral world presents itself as letters or annals read aloud or as in the case of Jeremiah 36, when the best preserver of an oracle turns out to be not the written text that is destroyed but the memory and capacity orally to [re-create] the message" (*Oral World and Written Word*, 133).

upon Babylon, that is, all these words which have been written concerning Babylon. Then Jeremiah said to Seraiah, 'As soon as you come to Babylon, then see that you read all these words aloud'" (51:60–61).[23] Literacy, for Jeremiah, was the safe encoding of prior sound; an encoding that was "frozen" until it became reanimated back into the world of sound.

The message from Jeremiah about the interplay of text and tongue is consistent: while sound is prior, the visual properties of text also serve Yahweh's purpose. Sound and sight work cooperatively. The scroll had portability that Jeremiah lacked. But Jeremiah had generative and regenerative power impossible for the scroll. God seems to use each for its role and in many cases uses both simultaneously. In the end, the scroll gets the last word because it can endure reliably even down to this day, while Jeremiah's life, of course, ended some time long ago.

Jesus on Text and Tongue (Third Period)

According to Matthew's summary, "When the crowds heard this, they were astonished at His teaching" (Matt. 22:33). Luke said it like this: "And all were speaking well of Him, and wondering at the gracious words which were falling from His lips" (Luke 4:22). John observed, "Never has a man spoken the way this man speaks" (John 7:46).

Summary statements like these portray the spoken words of Jesus as significantly central to his entire ministry. Even though the world had changed in seismic ways from Jeremiah to Christ, the oral way of processing information was still primary. How much literacy expanded between the sixth century BC and the time of Christ is debatable and far from precise. While many scholars have made optimistically generous estimates of widespread literacy, literacy expert William Harris's assessment suggests this wasn't the case. Recognizing that literacy itself is better charted on a continuum than as a litmus test, Harris

---

23 Given his typical employment of a scribe, it is difficult to determine whether this phrasing requires Jeremiah to have inscribed this message himself or whether a scribe is assumed.

estimates that only about 10 percent of the population of ancient Greece was literate in the sense we think of today.[24] That figure does not seem to change appreciably up through the Roman world of the first century AD.[25] Even though the elites of Greco-Roman culture were able to use literacy pervasively, they still relied on what orality scholar Walter Ong calls "oral residue" for the bulk of their social interaction.[26] He describes a tasteful blend of overlapping orality and literacy on the ancient palate.

But how did Jesus function in that ancient context? Where would his explicit statements and actual practice place him on the oral/literate continuum? Toward literacy we see him granting a high level of honor to the Law and the Prophets. "Not the smallest letter or stroke shall pass from the Law until all is accomplished" (Matt. 5:18). Yet the fact that he quotes them easily in the midst of everyday life shows a high value for oral fluency without dependence on an actual scroll. This is consistent with Matthew's description in 7:29: "For he was teaching them as one having authority, and not as their scribes." Scribal authority was based in text and textual expertise, including the pattern of citing which Rabbi is being consulted on a particular point of discussion. Scribes were accountants and compilers of outside information.[27] Jesus did not operate on that level since his teaching was *author*itative, characteristic of an author not a compiler of others' thoughts.[28]

---

24 Harris explains his rationale for this low percentage of literacy in ancient Greece as follows: "They frequently dictated letters instead of writing them for themselves; they listened to political news rather than reading it; they attended recitations and performances, or heard slaves reading, without having to read literary texts for themselves" (*Ancient Literacy*, 36).

25 Ibid., 61, 173.

26 Walter J. Ong, "Oral Residue in Tudor Prose Style," *PMLA* 80, no. 3 (1965): 145–54.

27 On the role of scribes in Judaism, see *Encyclopedia Judaica Online*, 2nd ed., s.v. "Scribe," by Aaron Demsky, accessed June, 22, 2014, http://www .bjeindy.org/resources/library/encyclopediajudaica/.

28 The Greek word for "authority" in Matthew 7:29 is *exousia* with the root meaning related to "power of choice" or "liberty of doing as one pleases." *Thayer's Greek Lexicon*, s.v. "*exousia*," accessed June, 22, 2014, http://

Jesus read the scroll of Isaiah in his hometown synagogue (Luke 4), and then moved smoothly into oral commentary on the reading. His parables embedded in everyday life have all the features of orality (Matthew 13), yet he never penned a word himself. By today's literate standards, it might seem odd that he left the writing to others, but it made perfect sense in his day, particularly as a respected rabbi. In fact it is because he was so respected, that writing—the province of mere scribes—would have been inconsistent with his role. This is why it never seems to strike his disciples or the early church as odd that they held no text from his hand.[29]

Jesus on Literacy

Despite the fact that Jesus chose not to write anything himself, he clearly expected some in his audience to be textually informed. In no less than six instances in Matthew alone, Jesus queried his skeptics with the probing question, "Have you never read?" He constantly appealed to Scripture as a body of knowledge that was authoritative and available to this educated upper class of priests, teachers of the law, and Pharisees. The written Word was, indeed, the repository of truth.

Matthew 22:29–32, addressing the Sadducees, is typical: "But Jesus answered and said to them, 'You are mistaken, not understanding the Scriptures nor the power of God. For in the

---

biblehub.com/thayers/1849.htm. Scribes didn't enjoy this liberty, as they were bound to copying content from original sources. In contrasting Jesus with scribes, Matthew is highlighting Jesus' role as generative rather than preservative.

29 Using Greek philosophers and their oratory for comparison, McLuhan discusses why such teachers as Socrates did not seek to be published in their day. He then goes on to quote a lengthy passage from Aquinas explaining why Jesus did not write: "First, on account of his own dignity; for the more excellent the teacher, the more excellent his manner of teaching ought to be. And therefore it was fitting that Christ, as the most excellent of teachers, should adopt that manner of teaching whereby his teaching would be imprinted on the hearts of his hearers" (*Summa Theologica* III, Q_42, A 4, co., quoted in *Gutenberg Galaxy*, 98).

resurrection they neither marry nor are given in marriage, but are like angels in heaven. But regarding the resurrection of the dead, have you not read what was spoken to you by God: "I am the God of Abraham, and the God of Isaac, and the God of Jacob"? He is not the God of the dead but of the living.'" Here is not just an expectation of literacy, but an argument based on the tense of two verbs.[30] Jesus is saying that the exact way the words were recorded is significant. This is precision literacy.

The expectation of literacy, however, was confined to the educated elite, and he nowhere demonstrated any such expectation of common folk. With them it was limited to the oral/aural environment as he began five sequential sections in Matthew's Sermon on the Mount with the observation: "You have heard that it was said . . . but I say to you."[31] Clearly their reception of the Word of God had been distorted by the literate minority who served as its gatekeepers. Jesus bypassed this elitism with confidence that commoners, though illiterate, were nevertheless capable of receiving a direct word from God.

Jesus on Orality

Despite the fact that Jesus displayed both literate and oral practice, the weight of his teaching tilted toward the oral delivery

---

30   The Greek verbs in verse 32 are *egō eimi* ("I myself am"), with the personal pronoun included and expressed only when emphatic as here, and *estin* ("he is"), both of which are present active in grammatical form. The Gospel writer is here quoting from the Septuagint (LXX), or Greek translation of the Old Testament, to convey Jesus' quotation of Exodus 3:6, which in the Hebrew Bible similarly includes the personal pronoun *'anoki* ("I") for emphasis. Originally, Jesus most likely quoted Exodus 3:6 in Hebrew (not in Greek), but otherwise was speaking to the Sadducees in Aramaic, the predominant language of Judea in the first century AD, a Semitic language similar to Hebrew dating back to when Aramaic was being spoken long before Judah went into exile. The Jews who returned to Jerusalem with Ezra and Nehemiah primarily spoke Aramaic, the language they and their children had learned in Babylon and continued speaking right up to Jesus' day.

31   Matthew 5:21, 27, 33, 38, 43.

of the Word of God. Consider the assumptions behind the hugely significant summary in Matthew 4, itself a quote from Deuteronomy 8:3. "Man shall not live on bread alone, but on every word that proceeds out of the mouth of God" (Matt. 4:4). It is not the pen of God, nor even the scroll of God. Revelation rolls off the divine tongue and through the divine lips. It is a categorical statement establishing the priority of the spoken word.

And when God speaks, it is we who are to hear. Jesus says nine times in the Gospels, "He who has ears to hear, let him hear."[32] He says hearing is foundational to obedience: "Everyone who hears these words of Mine and does not act on them, will be like a foolish man who built his house on the sand" (Matt. 7:26). Or consider Jesus' parable of the sower in Luke 8. The seed he describes as the Word of God and the soil is the hearer. After a brief parable about a lamp, Jesus concluded, "So take care how you listen; for whoever has, to him more shall be given; and whoever does not have, even what he thinks he has shall be taken away from him" (v. 18). It is in the listening process that the Word of God either finds root or is discarded. It is through the ear that the Word of God seeks a place to grow, and Jesus cautions the hearer to think carefully about the manner of listening.

This is consistent with the sheep/shepherd metaphor in John 10.

> But he who enters by the door is a shepherd of the sheep. To him the doorkeeper opens, and the sheep hear his voice, and he calls his own sheep by name and leads them out. When he puts forth all his own, he goes ahead of them, and the sheep follow him because they know his voice. A stranger they simply will not follow, but will flee from him, because they do not know the voice of strangers. (vv. 2–5)

Notice the sheep do not watch the shepherd and follow his example or scrutinize his appearance. Four times in a row the listening process is described as crucial to correctly identifying the

---

32   Matthew 11:15; 13:9, 43; Mark 4:9, 23; 7:16; 8:18; Luke 8:8; 14:35.

good shepherd. There is recognition of tone and texture of voice.[33] The sound of the voice carries personality even more than physical appearance. It is not uncommon to misidentify a friend in darkness or in disguise whereas we almost never mistake the voice of someone we know well. Jesus describes the ear as the most reliable authentication process in determining identity.

This priority of ear over eye to reveal character and personality is consistent with Jesus' other teaching about the importance of words in Luke 6:45: "The good man out of the good treasure of his heart brings forth what is good; and the evil man out of the evil treasure brings forth what is evil; for his mouth speaks from that which fills his heart." The mouth reliably reveals the heart. There is a connection between mouth and heart that cannot be as easily established in the world of literacy. We can pen all kinds of words we do not actually mean because the page removes the live context, effectively buffering and disguising the heart from its live expression. We can sign a card, "Love, Dad" insincerely, but who can avoid detection if the same phrase were to be voiced halfheartedly?

Jesus everywhere equated his ministry with his spoken words. They were not just the expression of who he was; they were his substance even as he bore the name "the Word." In the beginning of his ministry he prioritized his words: "Let us go somewhere else to the towns nearby, so that I may preach there also; for that is what I came for" (Mark 1:38). At the end of his life, his public teaching summarized his time on earth: "I have spoken openly to the world; I always taught in synagogues and in the temple, where all the Jews come together; and I spoke nothing in secret" (John 18:20). Significant portions of the Gospels are nothing more than his actual words, often in prolonged discourses of several chapters.[34] But not only did Jesus place high value on his own words, he expected the same sort of sensibility from his apostles.

Consider again his exhortation before sending out the twelve

---

33 In John 10, the Greek word for "voice," which occurs one time each in
    verses 3, 4, and 5, is *phōnē*, literally "sound" or "noise" (see also vv. 16, 27).
34 Matthew 23–25 and John 14–17, for example.

in Matthew 10. Words were to play a prominent role in their ministry. They were to preach, give greetings and blessings, testify under persecution, and proclaim things from the rooftops. Clearly their ministry was to be orally driven. They are never told to read or write anything, not even a single word. In what could be called the closest thing to homiletic theory that Jesus ever offered, he summarized what his disciples should expect in these words: "You will even be brought before governors and kings for My sake, as a testimony to them and to the Gentiles. But when they hand you over, do not worry about how or what you are to say; for it will be given you in that hour what you are to say. For it is not you who speak, but it is the Spirit of your Father who speaks in you" (vv. 18–20).

Jesus envisioned their ministry as oral. He advocated not an unbridled, purely expressive orality,[35] but one dependent upon divine guidance, even the guidance of the promised Spirit who will "guide you into all the truth" (John 16:13).

Paul on Text and Tongue (Fourth Period)

The epistles of Paul echo the same blend of literacy and orality we have seen so far. On the one hand, Paul had a great deal of confidence in the function of the written word to establish a binding and documented archive of truth. Commenting on the Old Testament in Romans 15, the apostle said, "For whatever was written in earlier times was written for our instruction, so that through perseverance and the encouragement of the Scriptures we might have hope" (v. 4). The abiding sense of the written word

---

35 In book 4 of *On Christian Doctrine*, Augustine comments on this balance between preparation and speaking extempore: "And for this reason, he who would both know and teach should learn everything which should be taught and acquire a skill in speaking appropriate to an ecclesiastic, but at the time of the speech itself he should think that which the Lord says more suitable to good thought: 'Take no thought how or what to speak: for it shall be given you in that hour what to speak. For it is not you that speak, but the Spirit of your Father that speaketh in you'" (4.15.32). For Augustine, there is a time to prepare and a time to forget about preparing.

can live beyond any single generation and provide continuity and comfort. Similarly, Paul said in 1 Corinthians 10, "Now these things happened to them as an example, and they were written for our instruction, upon whom the ends of the ages have come" (v. 11). Warnings need a sense of permanence that literacy can provide.

That Paul considered the sacred texts of Judaism authoritative is patently obvious by his frequent (thirty-one times) use of the phrase, "It is written" in reference to the Old Testament.[36] The written record was a repository of timeless truth that could be cited as evidence. Consider what Paul said in 1 Corinthians 15:54: "But when this perishable will have put on the imperishable, and this mortal will have put on immortality, then will come about the saying that is written, 'Death is swallowed up in victory.'" This role of text here is itself an old blend of oral and literate where the "saying" becomes "written" as the seer or prophet takes up the pen. But, consistent with the pattern, the saying precedes the writing.

Of course the very fact that Paul's letters were themselves written and delivered in text argues for Paul's extensive use of writing. First Corinthians 5:9 is typical: "I wrote you in my letter not to associate with immoral people." It is not uncommon at all for Paul to write about his writing. Indeed, in 2 Corinthians 10 he complains loudly (if a pen can be considered loud) about the misunderstandings fostered by letter writing: "For I do not wish to seem as if I would terrify you by my letters. For they say, 'His letters are weighty and strong, but his personal presence is unimpressive and his speech contemptible.' Let such a person consider this, that what we are in word by letters when absent, such persons we are also in deed when present" (vv. 9–11). Preferring to be present, Paul nevertheless understands

---

36 The Greek verb for "it is written" is *gegraptai*, and is perfect passive in grammatical form, emphasizing completed action with enduring effects. The texts of Scripture that existed at this time (i.e., the Old Testament, which as far as the writers of the New Testament were concerned was the Bible of Jesus and the apostles) are almost always referenced in the New Testament in this perfect tense, emphasizing their ongoing authority.

that a letter, while imperfect, is better than nothing, and that misperceptions will be eventually cleared up in the context of face-to-face communication.

In many ways Paul's concern here echoes that of Plato some four hundred years earlier when he described a written document as an orphan lacking fatherly protection. It's not difficult to conclude there's a consistent respect and valid role for both the spoken word and for written text in the history of God's people.[37] One can see both sides reflected in Paul's closing admonition to the Thessalonians: "So then, brethren, stand firm and hold to the traditions which you were taught, whether by word of mouth or by letter from us" (2 Thess. 2:15). But, the pattern seems to be that words are first presented in speech and then preserved in writing.[38]

Water → Ice → Water

God's Word as originally spoken was like living water to the generation who first heard and acted upon it. But water, while being perfect for consumption, is difficult to transport because of its tendency to leak or evaporate. To transport water over long distances and time frames, it is expedient to freeze it in literacy.

Sacred text is like frozen revelation—well preserved, but silent

---

37 Here biblical scholars sensitive to orality might protest literate bias even in this uncovering of oral foundations. To maintain a feasible scope, the analysis in this chapter was entirely textual/visual/content-based and strategically neglected the sound patterns, oral formulas, epithets, and repetitions that strongly suggest an oral composition for much of Scripture. For a more "sonic" exemplary analysis of the words of the text, see the work already mentioned by Susan Niditch, *Oral World and Written Word: Ancient Israelite Literature* (Louisville: Westminster John Knox, 1996), and Richard A. Horsley, Jonathan A. Draper, and John Miles Foley, eds., *Performing the Gospel: Orality, Memory, and Mark; Essays Dedicated to Werner Kelber* (Minneapolis: Fortress, 2006).

38 Niditch observes the corollary interplay between written and oral works: "At the same time, however, writing offers the opportunity to preserve orally created and employed compositions. Aspects of the literate end of the continuum clearly shape and influence oral works as well. Written works, in turn, may be reoralized and the new works then written down, and so on" (*Oral World and Written Word*, 133).

and difficult to consume. Preachers, then, receive this frozen mass and have the responsibility to warm it again and serve it anew as a timeless word reentering time. It is not our own word, but we use our own words in the melting.

For this reason, Stephen Webb in *The Divine Voice* argues that even in modernity the best place to hear the Word of God is in church,[39] and that all the frozen blocks of sacred text resident in homes and libraries cannot replace the shared hearing of the Word of God, the way in which the melted water of God comes simultaneously and corporately to God's people by the carefully heated sermon and the suitably warmed preacher.

---

39   Webb, *Divine Voice*, 208.

6

TONGUE BEFORE TEXT

Introduction to Orality

Until we learn the use of living words we shall continue to be
waxworks inhabited by gramophones.

Walter de La Mare, "Sayings of the Week," *The Observer*

In 1891 Thomas Edison and his assistant William Dickson stunned the world with a demonstration of their revolutionary new machines: a Kinetograph to capture a rapid sequence of still photographs, and a companion Kinetoscope that enabled the viewer to see, for the first time, those still pictures dancing in what appeared to be motion.[1] Until that point, action had always been impossible to capture. As hard as it is to imagine now in the era of rewind and fast-forward, once an event occurred back then it would never be seen again. Action could occur only in the present. But Edison made the simulated action repeatable and preservable. For the first time, sight could be archived. Edison and his technological successors changed the way we think about life, which could now be endlessly captured and replayed.

The Oral World Upended

Thousands of years ago, a similar innovation changed the way humans interacted. From the dawn of civilization, speech had

---

1   Neil Baldwin, *Edison: Inventing the Century* (1995; Chicago: University of Chicago Press, 2001), 221.

always been impossible to capture. Once spoken, words, unless memorized, were lost forever. But it was not the tape recorder that produced this first upheaval. It was something even more innovative, but strangely routine for us today: the alphabet, developed around 1500 BC.[2]

Before the alphabet, sound could not be charted. Though people spoke with precision and intelligence, they were what we would call today, illiterate. But as civilizations became more organized, documentation became necessary. Starting as scratches and then pictures, early scribes transferred concepts onto clay or stones to record payments, inventories, and legal contracts.[3] These simple pictures quickly became broadly recognized symbols that represented actual items.

Gradually symbols began to stand for individual syllables. For example, they would combine, in modern English equivalence, a symbol for "dog" and an adjacent symbol for "mother" to forge and render the word (or more properly, the sound) "dogma" (which has no relation to either dogs or motherhood, but is an entirely new blend of the two).[4] Pictures were starting to lose their tight correspondence with actual physical items and adopt a looser, more symbolic meaning. Symbols were starting to encompass complex and abstract ideas. But the real breakthrough was yet to come: the alphabet.

Immersed as we are in literacy, we seldom realize how revolutionary the alphabet was. Sounds began to be mapped and recorded economically and accurately with phonetic rather than pictographic encoding. With a wonderfully simple collection of roughly twenty alphabetic letters, almost any noise the human mouth could enunciate could be both coded and decoded.

This had seismic implications. Think about it. For the first time,

---

2   Ong, *Orality and Literacy*, 88.

3   Schökel, *Inspired Word*, 245.

4   The technical term for this use of pictographs is *rebus* writing. See chapter 4 in Ong's *Orality and Literacy*, or Thomas F. Bertonneau, "Orality, Literacy, and the Tradition," *Modern Age* 45, no. 2 (2003): 113–22, for a concise historical overview of the development of the alphabet.

people could read and pronounce other people's words. Up until that point, every speaker had only his own words to work with. Now, without having to memorize anything, speakers could mimic the words of others, and audiences were confronted, for the first time, with secondhand (even borrowed or plagiarized) thoughts. Suddenly sound—words—had an archive, and human thought and communicative interaction would never be the same.[5]

Plato did a considerable amount of hand-wringing over this innovation. Although, ironically, scholars have concluded that Plato was responsible for a good deal of the shift toward literacy, he also harbored grave misgivings about the concept.[6] In a sort of double irony, we only know of these misgivings about writing because he chose to document those misgivings in writing.[7] Plato was concerned that writing would become the doorway to artifice and duplicity. He compared the written text to an orphan detached from its author/parent.

But despite Plato's warning, literacy and literate ways of thinking came to dominate Western culture from that time forward.

---

5   As amazing as the alphabet is, Schökel points out the remaining limitations. While the alphabet can capture one facet of communication, namely diction, musical scores are actually much more sound sensitive in their ability to capture pitch, volume, and rhythm on paper (*Inspired Word*, 272).

6   Ong quotes classicist Eric Havelock extensively on the point of Plato's ironic undermining of orality even as he celebrated it (*Orality and Literacy*, 79). See Eric A. Havelock, *The Muse Learns to Write: Reflections on Orality and Literacy from Antiquity to the Present* (New Haven, CT: Yale University Press, 1988), 1–19.

7   In the dialogue between Socrates and Phaedrus, Plato has Socrates say at one point, "Writing, Phaedrus, has this strange quality, and is very like painting; for the creatures of painting stand like living beings, but if one asks them a question, they preserve a solemn silence. And so it is with written words; you might think they spoke as if they had intelligence, but if you question them, wishing to know about their sayings, they always say only one and the same thing. And every word, when once it is written, is bandied about, alike among those who understand and those who have no interest in it, and it knows not to whom to speak or not to speak; when ill-treated or unjustly reviled it always needs its father to help it; for it has no power to protect or help itself." Plato, *Phaedrus* 1:565, 567 (Fowler, LCL).

Indeed, the rise of modernity itself was facilitated by the ability of each generation to document their contributions to the overall accumulation of knowledge and build upon it. Literacy literally built the West.

During the 1960s, however, a growing dissatisfaction with modernity surfaced in many avenues of culture. The twentieth century, with its orientation toward certainty and objective scientific knowledge had succeeded in delivering seemingly unstoppable technological advances. Yet two world wars testified to humanity's continued inability to find meaning or govern lives any better than the ancient world, which was grounded in authority and tradition. Modernity could produce a microwaved cup of coffee, but could not deliver a person with whom to share it, or a reason for the conversation. There was unsettledness all around, and openness to revisit positions that were more natural, organic, unmediated by modernity.

In this milieu, Jesuit priest Walter Ong emerged as the spokesman for a neglected era—the age before the printing press when human speech was still primary in the human experience.[8] As a communication scholar as well as a priest he sensed the theological implications of orality and literacy for the study and preaching of God's revelation (what he calls "the Word"). He unpacked those implications in three volumes, framing the Bible both as a product of literacy and as an experience of God's presence in the orally spoken word.[9] Ong believed the world needed to recover something it once enjoyed but had lost along the road to modernity.

---

8   Ong, *Presence of the Word*, 6.
9   These three volumes by Walter J. Ong, chronologically listed, include the already-cited *The Presence of the Word: Some Prolegomena for Cultural and Religious History* (New Haven, CT: Yale University Press, 1967); *Interfaces of the Word: Studies in the Evolution of Consciousness and Culture* (Ithaca, NY: Cornell University Press, 1977); and *Orality and Literacy: The Technologizing of the Word* (New York: Routledge, 1982). All subsequent citations for these volumes are those listed here except citations to *Orality and Literacy* are from the previously cited Routledge second edition (2002).

Ancient Hebrews and Christians knew not only the spoken word but the alphabet as well, as their devotion to the sacred scriptures makes plain. But for them and all men of early times, the Word, even when written, was much closer to the spoken word than it normally is for twentieth-century technological man. Today we have often to labor to regain the awareness that the word is still always at root the spoken word. Early man had no such problem: he felt the word, even when written, as primarily an event in sound.[10]

In attempting this recovery, Ong took on the difficult assignment of demonstrating to moderns a premodern understanding of the world. Turning back the clock and calendar, he attempted to peel back our unreflective reliance upon the world of sight and print to reanimate the older world of sound and speech. To do so, he needed to predate even Greek understandings and recover a Hebrew mindset: "The Hebrews tended to think of understanding as a kind of hearing, whereas the Greeks thought of it more as a kind of seeing."[11]

Ong postulated three stages of development in our ability to receive and process information: (1) the unrecorded word (oral culture), (2) the denatured word (alphabet and print), and (3) the electronic word (recorded sound and "secondary" orality).[12] Central in his argument is the constant reminder of the artificial and technological nature of literacy. He repeatedly reminds us that people functioned quite well for thousands of years before literacy was commonplace. Moderns tend to think of the pen and keyboard as organic extensions of the human hand, as natural as the fingers themselves. Ong labors to overthrow this equation of literacy with intelligence, reminding us that if preliterate people were so dumb, how did they ever invent writing? Even naming them as "pre-

---

10   Ong, *Presence of the Word*, xxvii.
11   Ibid., 3. From Origen on, church fathers began to emphasize seeing over hearing, shifting the sensorium toward Greek philosophical orientations (Wilken, *Spirit of Early Christian Thought*, 20).
12   Ong, *Presence of the Word*, 17.

literate" frames them in a deficiency they never felt themselves—
similar to labeling a horse as a "pre-car."[13]

By patiently rewinding the history of technology, Ong takes
us back to the point where people had no way to archive sound.
Every speech act was unique and contextualized, what Ong calls
"unrepeatable." It is not as if people chose not to take notes
or document proceedings or write letters, but that they were
unable to—they lacked that technology just as surely as they
lacked a microwave oven. Yet just as surely as there was cooking
before microwaves, primarily oral cultures still enjoyed theology
and ethics and community and shared meaning. In what seems
an almost blasphemous notion to print-driven culture, Ong
argues that all the essential elements of human endeavor can
work without literacy. Indeed, of the more than three thousand
spoken languages today, only about seventy-eight have produced
literature.[14] The rest remain primarily oral. God made us oral as
part of creating us in his image. Language is an aspect of the image
of God. Language is also the basis of culture. We hear because
God hears; we speak because God speaks. Yet our use of literacy,
while precious, is less central to our identity as humans than we
may think.

How They Used to Do It

Ong does much more than describe what has been lost in the
move from primary orality toward literacy. He also re-creates what
he calls the "psychodynamics" of orality. To grasp the world of
orality in fullness, we are continually challenged to stop knowing
what it seems we have always known. Ong asks us to imagine,
admittedly with some difficulty, a world with no writing, and more
importantly, no knowledge of the possibility of writing. In such a
setting every word would be a sound and only a sound.

When we hear the noise[15] "door" expressed, we can barely hear
or pronounce it without its complementary language partner, the

---

13   Ibid., 13.
14   Ibid., 7.
15   The technical term for a word as a sound is *phoneme*.

alphabetic sequence of a *d*, two *o*s, and an *r*, coming to mind. But that connection, Ong tells us, is learned and artificial. It would be possible and indeed was commonplace to link the sound "door" only to its physical reality. Early efforts to capture the concept "door" in text resorted to pictographic representations—a tiny door drawn on paper. But we can quickly spot the inefficiency of the pictographic system that requires as many pictures as there are things (as well as the inconvenience of trying to configure nonmaterial concepts like fear or loyalty).

The genius of the alphabet was that it mapped sound with amazing economy by reducing every sound to a combination of symbols evoking a particular noise. Add all the separate noises together and speed them up phonetically, and you have a spoken word captured. Then learn to associate visually the sequence of written letters ("door") with the actual door on its hinges, and you have, in two steps, invented a work-around for audible communication. This work-around, which initially must have seemed virtually miraculous, became so commonplace that it feels normal, even native to us. But Ong asks us to imagine a culture where there is no dictionary to look things up: "In a primary oral culture, the expression 'to look something up' is an empty phrase: it would have no conceivable meaning. Without writing, words as such have no visual presence, even when the objects they represent are visual."[16] There is a physical door. There is the sound "door" as spoken. But there is no spelled-out alphabetic word.

Shedding what you already know is difficult, especially when you are shedding literacy, and using literacy in the process of attempting to shed it. Part of this stepping back could be accomplished better in person, but we're not. So we use this book as a better-than-nothing tool.

In his summary work *Orality and Literacy*, Ong documents nine characteristics of oral communication, many of which will be applicable to homiletics in the crafting of a sermon that is as orally adept as it is textually grounded. Interestingly enough, though

---

16 Ong, *Orality and Literacy*, 31.

Ong applies orality scholarship to various disciplines, including literary history, anthropology, sociology, philosophy, and biblical studies,[17] he stops short of making any explicit connections between orality and homiletics—despite the fact that as a priest he would have preached regularly. For some reason he left this task to others.

So let's use the Ong time machine to step back into the world in which God's Word was originally delivered, the world of the apostles and prophets. Ong calls these the psychodynamics of orality, but it really just means how people communicated. The titles of his terms are rather technical, but the ideas are simple.[18]

Imprecise

Ong points to the way that oral discourse falls out in awkward syntax without clearly defined sequence. Speech tends to connect phrases with simple *and*s instead of organizational *next*s, *because*s, or *then*s. This is because the live context often supplies the sequence in such a way that it is not necessary to state. Real speech is full of interruptions, unfinished clauses, interjections, amplifications, and other things the literate world considers clumsy. Writing (and editing) irons out all the clumsiness and seeks to orient each sentence and clause smoothly.

In homiletics, the manuscript or printed sermon typically includes no interjections, running sentences, or awkward fragments, for they are almost impossible to plan, being naturally produced in the moment. If the preacher excludes those from the sermon, the effect is fluid and smooth, but it moves the sermon out of the genre of discovery and into the world of reporting. There is a price to pay either way. The unpolished speech full of comparative oral clumsiness might suffer a lack of precision

---

17 Ibid., 157–70.

18 In doing so, I've simplified and/or paraphrased these psychodynamic categories to make them more approachable. Ong's more technical labels are found in chapter 3 of *Orality and Literacy*.

or credibility with certain audiences.[19] But the polished sermon suffers a distance from the audience that can cripple it in another direction.

Formulaic

Ong here refers to an accumulation of oral word "clusters" that seem to travel together. We find this in English when certain words are used almost always with other partner words. If someone says "nigh unto" we know the next word is likely either "death" or "impossible." There are phonological patterns engrained in speech that the mind expects to hear.

In Israel, oral liturgical resources such as the Shema worked this way. Once the oral pattern started (e.g., "Hear, O Israel! . . ."), there was no doubt as to what came next. In the New Testament, Jesus employed a variety of oral formulas, including "Truly, truly I say to you, . . ." "He who has ears to hear, let him hear," and "The kingdom of heaven is at hand."

Theologically this occurs in the church when oral formulas are used to reinforce theological concepts. When we refer to things like "eternal life" or the "blessed hope" or the "last days," we invoke familiar patterns of speech that conjure up more to the audience than the sum of the individual words. There is a formulaic sense to them that is shared and traditional and can be either powerful or trite or alienating, depending on how they are utilized. Commonly utilized recitations like the Lord's Prayer or the Twenty-Third Psalm have formulaic patterns, and the more liturgical the church, the more oral patterns will recur in worship, in part because orality and liturgy were closely connected in the generally preliterate time period of the early church. Though oral formulas can become routine, even mundane, orally oriented preachers recognize the power of formulaic expressions—even in the midst of a sermon—tapping into the sound sequence of shared key words to build a sense of community.

---

19 The framing of orality as "unpolished" and "clumsy" anticipates the bias of literacy against imprecision. From an older perspective, one might just as well call literacy "artificial," "detached," or "lifeless."

Redundant

Redundancy, normally a taboo in written culture, is necessary in orality. Even Ong's own categories of these very psychodynamics bear this sense of overlap and repetition. He explains that readers can always go back to reread something they missed.[20] The writer doesn't have to "wait" for the reader. But the speaker has no such luxury since the audience cannot "backloop" at will. So the preacher must repeat creatively what has already been said to allow the listener another chance to grasp something first missed.

Ecclesiastes, which was likely spoken before it was written, exhibits this oral repetition: the themes of the brevity of life, the futility of wealth, the value of work, and accountability to the Creator come up not once but in regularly repeating cycles.[21] Preachers looking for a systematic approach to the book are no doubt frustrated by this would-be literary oversight in organization. But Solomon, who calls himself "The Preacher," is unrepentantly oral and therefore repetitive.

Homiletically speaking, the oral impulse allows us to loop through the same content repeatedly and does not require each thought to be spoken only once. Redundancy is utilized, even celebrated. This opens the door for a preacher to "read" the room and repeat or reinforce as needed until there is a sense of shared understanding.

Conversely, a precrafted sermon will tend to rely on a concise outline that proceeds in orderly fashion at a pace determined by the content, not the audience. It might be objected that if the outline is published either on paper or screen, the listener can "backloop" as necessary, and that's a good point. But it seems unwise to invite your audience to check in and out of the sermon at will, pacing their own independent experience of the sermon with their own literary version of "remote control."

---

20   Ong, *Orality and Literacy*, 40.
21   From its title (literally, "The Preacher") to its themes, to its composition, Ecclesiastes bears many of these hallmarks of oral culture.

Tradition Driven

Although the idea of an orally driven sermon might seem innovative, Ong argues that an oral culture is more traditional and conservative than a literate culture. This is not a political or economic conservatism, but a communal impulse toward preserving long-standing values. If text preserves speech, orality preserves values. There is a difference between consulting a book and consulting the wise old elders in the village.[22] Oral culture not only values the past, but feels a duty to pass it down, even as in Proverbs where the father longs to see his son embrace the traditional values of wisdom.[23] The oral sermon does not inform as much as it does inspire the congregation to uphold and act out already-held and shared beliefs.

Close to Everyday Life

Oral cultures are experientially driven in the sense that they do not concern themselves with theoretical or hypothetical knowledge. It is contextualized knowledge that belongs in a particular place, with and to a particular people. They do not primarily talk about fishing in a universal sense (as in what does all fishing have in common, or what might be the timeless principles of fishing). When they talk about fishing, it is more likely to be about fishing in this pond by this person to catch this kind of fish on this day.

It is striking that the revelation of God is in this same way so close to the world of human life. A good portion of the New Testament's revelation is comprised of epistles written to actual churches or individuals. For the most part the apostles did not write to some imagined church universal, but to specific congrega-

---

22 Ong was suspicious of the ways that print culture unseats legitimate authority: "By storing knowledge outside the mind, writing and, even more, print downgrades the figures of the wise old man and wise old woman, repeaters of the past, in favor of younger discoverers of something new" (Ong, *Orality and Literacy*, 41).

23 The first five chapters of Proverbs set up this traditionalist approach to wisdom from an oral perspective. Wisdom "calls out" to the young man and warns him repeatedly to "listen" to the experience of the elders.

tions whose lives and contexts they knew well. Twenty-one centuries later we still read, in his last letter to Timothy his son in the
faith, the apostle Paul's very earthy request for scrolls and a coat he
had left with Carpus at Troas (2 Tim. 4:13).

Homiletically, the oral sermon cannot escape universal and
timeless truth, nor should it try. But it can approach that truth
in the context of an actual congregation in an actual town
facing actually known issues.[24] The sermon is addressed to
this congregation in specific, and could not be dropped into
another congregation in another town without substantial loss of
meaning. Today it is common to think of sermons as universally
applicable that can be broadcast or downloaded or exported to any
congregation in America. But if the same sermon can go anywhere,
to what extent did it consider the actual flock in residence? To
what extent should it be "their" sermon?

Familiar with Suffering

Oral cultures frame themselves in heroic struggles against
common foes. Life is an uphill battle that must be seriously
engaged. Public speech is like a report from the front lines of the
battle, a combination of pep rally and challenge. African American
sermons typically embody this kind of joint-struggle metaphor.[25]
But precrafted sermons without an audience in mind, lose the
sense of collective struggle.

---

24 The scriptural letters of Paul are simultaneously specific and universal;
    addressed to the whole world, but also to specific recipients; timeless, yet
    still very temporal. Though temporal expressions can have eternal relevance,
    the original audience undoubtedly got the most pungent expression.
    In oral composition the concrete audience not only has the front-row
    seat, but also exerts a participatory influence, keeping the expression
    phenomenologically grounded. That is, preacher and congregation are
    sharing not just hypothetical truths ("God is always with us") but also
    experiential truth ("God seems to leave us alone at key moments").

25 Cleopas LaRue describes the role of joint suffering: "The distinctly black
    experience of marginalization and struggle is crucial to understanding
    what gives depth and dimension to black preaching" (LaRue, *Heart of
    Black Preaching*, 121).

We can see this perseverance through suffering in places like Psalm 105 and 106. Both describe the cooperative struggles of Israel against their enemies. The Psalms, an oral resource of shared hymns, often frame Israel in a multigenerational struggle to maintain community faithfulness to the covenant. The mindset is "we" and "us" and "our God." The prophets make similar appeals to national as opposed to individual righteousness.[26] A theology of suffering is common in the New Testament as well. That doesn't always appeal to a culture obsessed with health and happiness, but it's part of how humans embrace the vulnerability and shortness of life. An oral preacher develops and articulates a rich theology of suffering for the benefit of the body.

Participatory

Oral cultures define themselves as part of a "people." Their individual boats rise and fall with the community tide.[27] As in many of the previous characteristics of oral culture, the issue of community is unavoidable. Literacy typically builds the individual and promotes individual interests and concepts of self, even as a text can be read silently to oneself. Orality always builds community and a corporate sense of self since words must be spoken out loud to a common audience. That alone is reason enough to bring orality back to preaching.

Every preacher has to choose how to apply the sermon: to individuals or to the corporate body. Since literate Americans are highly individual, most sermons are applied to individuals. You, as an individual, should do this or that. Your individual relationship

---

26 Examples of this are too numerous to cite. But take for instance Jeremiah's opening salvo in his indictment of Israel and notice the corporate sense of sin: "For My people have committed two evils: they have forsaken Me, the fountain of living waters, to hew for themselves cisterns: broken cisterns that can hold no water" (2:13).

27 Ong describes the role of a community-based consciousness in these terms: "The objectivity which Homer and other oral performers do have is that enforced by formulaic expression: the individual's reaction is not expressed as simply individual or 'subjective' but rather as encased in the communal reaction, the 'communal soul'" (Ong, *Orality and Literacy*, 46).

to God needs this or that. Your individual struggle against cancer or doubt or gossip means this or that. Very rarely do we apply a text of Scripture to the whole congregation. "We need to do this." "We have neglected this or that." That may be a reflection not only of how individualized we are as Americans, but how functionally independent we are from each other's ups and downs. Should our life together as the church, with the struggles and challenges each one faces, be so compartmentalized and disconnected from each other during the week? It is something we need to explore more deeply.

United in Purpose

Oral communities maintain identity by continually remembering the right things: "Oral societies live very much in a present which keeps itself in equilibrium or homeostasis by sloughing off memories which no longer have present relevance."[28] Perhaps the best biblical illustrations are the imprecatory psalms. In these we clearly see a partisan orientation in this oral culture. The enemies of Israel are the enemies of God, and their destiny is not contemplated with civility. There is no fair and balanced appraisal in an imprecatory psalm, but rather an unapologetic call for punishment.[29]

You cannot very well lead a pep rally by presenting a fair and balanced analysis of both teams on the field. Pep rallies take sides and unapologetically so. The oral preacher takes the side of the church, and the sermon in some respects accomplishes the same purpose. Oral preaching is loyal to the church, defends her from other interested opponents, and seeks the welfare of the church even as it addresses internal problems. Loyalties are never in doubt.

---

28   Ibid., 46.

29   See Psalm 69 for an extended example: "For they have persecuted him whom You Yourself have smitten, and they tell of the pain of those whom You have wounded. Add iniquity to their iniquity, and may they not come into Your righteousness. May they be blotted out of the book of life and may they not be recorded with the righteous" (vv. 26–28).

Comfortable with Stories

Oral people tend to see truth in the context of story. Their values do not flow from abstract rational principles, but from the wisdom of actual lived experience. We can see this in Jesus' heavy reliance upon parables and story in his teaching.[30] His universal applications are drawn out of specific stories, leaving no wedge between truth and life. The more literate we are, the less connected we are to story. Stories were how we organized ideas without ink. After ink, we didn't need stories as much because the page itself served as an organizational tool. The written page was the first visual aid and it quickly began to erode our need for story as the glue of an idea.

The difference in actual thinking patterns of oral and literate people is palpable, and Ong used it to begin to point out how literacy actually "restructures consciousness." In other words, once the ways of literacy are learned, it is impossible to go back, because certain modes of thinking (like using story to define a group) are lost like an atrophied muscle. Once we learn to see knowledge printed on page and external to any human "host," it becomes difficult to erase that notion and return to oral innocence. Ong's critique is strong, but there is no denying that literacy changes how we think about knowledge. With literacy, knowledge acquires a slipperiness and portability that is simply alarming to an oral community. It becomes not only universal, but generic. It can escape and travel without permission from the originating author.[31]

So how does this affect the preacher? We have noted there was a time when no one would have said, "My sermon is there on the table." Objectifying it like that frames it as something outside the preacher. Literacy allows sermons to move out on their own: to

---

30   Matthew cannot state this strongly enough: "All these things Jesus spoke to the crowds in parables, and He did not speak to them without a parable" (13:34).

31   This, of course, was Plato's original anxiety. Once people could read, they could also speak words that never originated in their own minds, with potentially dangerous hypocrisies. See earlier discussion in this chapter.

books, and satellite, and Internet. It can also finish a sermon so it no longer responds to a room or a particular time and place. Erase the name of the author and it can be completely anonymous: written by no one in particular, to anyone, who lives anywhere. Ong would suggest that the best definition of a sermon is the live event where it is uttered by a person to persons in a specific context and shared space. In that sense, while a record of the sermon may survive in some form, the actual sermon was and is unrepeatable.

This is not to say that Ong was hostile to literacy. He never denigrates the strategic use of literacy, and never wishes nostalgically to try to live without it. As a scholar of unbelievable breadth, his work survives today only because of the strengths of literacy. After all, he wrote and published books. His call was never for its elimination, but for its balance with the strengths of earlier oral resources. This is important as we anticipate an orally agile preacher who, like the process of revelation itself, utilizes the partnership of both orality and literacy.

Literacy Gone Wild

A thorough reading of Walter Ong leaves the impression that his concern is not the mere invention of writing, but the damage done by unbridled mass literacy. It was not the invention of the alphabet and the ability to map sound. That achievement made possible the crucial documentation of history and theology. Handwritten documents served a vital role for the educated and designated preservers of a culture, and represented only positive change.[32] Originally, text was not for generating ideas, but to preserve them after being spoken. It was a tool for scribes, priests, and diplomats. But the high cost and advanced education it required placed a limit on how much mass influence writing enjoyed.

The average Israelite farmer, Greek soldier, and first-century Christian slave, while reverencing text as valuable or even sacred, could not have imagined owning their own library or reading bedtime stories to their children, much less writing their own

---

32   Ong's term is "chirographic."

letters or journals. Even medieval monks who spent a good portion of their lives copying manuscripts still lived in communities with tremendous oral underpinnings, so much so that they were reportedly only semiliterate even though they produced vast amounts of artistically charged hand-copied literature.[33] Reading hand-copied literature was commonly done out loud and to an audience; a shared experience, not a private one. As long as writing was used to preserve speech, it maintained balance since the actual preparation and delivery was based in orality.[34]

This is an important feature of what we might call a "bilingual" sermon; one that is shaped by text and potentially preserved in text, but one whose structure is a product of voice and dialogue. You probably do this if you write out your sermons. You instinctively write with an oral style. We might even call it oral writing.

The Printing Press and Hyperliteracy

But to fully grasp Ong's point we need to hear him on the impact of the printing press. Ong's mentor and friend Marshall McLuhan published the *Gutenberg Galaxy* in 1962, just about the time Ong was ruminating over the oral/literate duality that swept through Europe in the sixteenth century.[35]

---

33 Douglas Burton-Christie, "Listening, Reading, and Praying: Orality, Literacy and Early Monastic Spirituality," *Anglican Theological Review* 83, no. 2 (2001): 208.

34 Ong notes the way sound preceded text: "Early written poetry everywhere, it seems, is at first necessarily a mimicking in script of oral performance. The mind has initially no properly chirographic resources. You scratch out on a surface words you imagine yourself saying aloud in some realizable oral setting. Only very gradually does writing become composition in writing, a kind discourse—poetic or otherwise—that is put together without a feeling that the one writing is actually speaking aloud (as early writers may well have done in composing)" (Ong, *Orality and Literacy*, 26).

35 Ong repeatedly makes clear his dependence on McLuhan, the noted Canadian communications theorist and professor of English literature: "His cardinal gnomic saying, 'The medium is the message,' registered his acute awareness of the importance of the shift from orality to literacy and

McLuhan's classic work on these kinds of technological shifts, like much of Ong's work, is a paradox itself. There is always irony in writing about writing, but McLuhan had the especially awkward task of using print culture to critique print culture.[36] Ong explains this by saying that whenever a technology has been thoroughly infused into a culture, critiques of that latest technology often employ that same technology in the critique. So if you don't like what television is doing to human interaction, you might choose to film a TV documentary that explains the dangers.

Ong's concerns with print culture center on the finished sense that print gives to any author's material. When writing was handwritten, the text was still a record of primary sound, and the underlying assumption was that it required a reader to reanimate the sound. A manuscript was viewed as we might view a CD today. We know the sound is "on there," but it takes a CD player to unleash it. The reader was like the CD player. We would not think of an "unplayed" CD as having much value. A handwritten manuscript was not finished until it was read out loud. While silent reading was technically possible, it was the printing press with its unprecedented potential that launched silent reading on a massive scale.[37] Today we think of silent reading as the norm. We do it all the time without even thinking. But silent reading is a

---

from print to electronic media. Few people have had so stimulating an effect as Marshall McLuhan on so many diverse minds, including those who disagreed with him or believed they did" (ibid., 29).

36 There is a sort of quiet mutiny, though, even in the printing of the *Gutenberg Galaxy*. Lacking any breakdown of chapters, headings, or subtitles, the book proceeds at a breathless pace looping backward and forward through centuries of diverse scholarship. McLuhan's authorship is more like a narration, embodying, as no accident, a more oral than literate structure.

37 We can almost hear Ong's disgust with print culture as he contrasts it with "chirographic control of space" like that of beautiful handwritten calligraphy: "Typographic control typically impresses more by its tidiness and inevitability: the lines perfectly regular, all justified on the right side, everything coming out even visually, and without the aid of the guidelines or ruled borders that often occur in manuscripts. This is an insistent world of cold, non-human, facts" (Ong, *Orality and Literacy*, 120).

huge shift from the ancient world of the Bible.

Since today's Bibles are printed by the million, they have a visual orderliness, a sense of standardization, an almost mechanical nature. Though we don't often realize it, the "bookish" nature of our Bibles is a significant change in how we experience the Word of God when compared to previous handwritten eras. We have already noted how the change of format from book to smartphone will again change how people experience God's Word. What does it mean, for instance, when God's Word runs out of batteries? While we are not saying that mass printing of the Bible has had a negative effect, its tidy depersonalized presentation does affect how its message comes across.

Orality and Theology: The Cost of Unbalanced Literacy

It is not coincidental that this concern for orality springs from a theologian. Ong has much more in mind than merely the charming recovery of an earlier communicative age. At stake is how God's revelation erupts among us and how we process and recommunicate that revelation.[38] Ong is convinced that certain characteristics of orality are close to the very mouth and mind of God, and that those who purport to carry the divine word in a merely literate box lose something of the richness and personality of "the Word." This is not to disparage the literate nature of revelation or literacy as a gift from God,[39] but to balance the notable strengths of literacy with a largely forgotten and unappreciated theological orality.

Loss of Revelatory Presence

There are a number of casualties in forgetting the oral roots of Scripture. Ong has concerns that an unbalanced theological

---

38 Ong scholar Paul Soukoup has connected Ong's religious presuppositions to his orality scholarship in "Contexts of Faith: The Religious Foundation of Walter Ong's Literacy and Orality," *Journal of Media and Religion* 5, no. 3 (2006): 175–88.

39 Ong, *Presence of the Word*, 314.

literacy forgets or neglects the intensity of God's presence in sound. This presence boils down to the essential difference between the worlds of sight and sound. Because sight is spatial, it can freeze in time as a snapshot captures a visual image. You can study the image indefinitely. Sound is different. It cannot be frozen and must exist only in time as an ephemeral expression of personal force: "Sound signals the present use of power, since sound must be in active production in order to exist at all."[40] Sounds call us to awareness of the very present "here and now" existence of another person. Ong illustrates appropriately: "A primitive hunter can see, feel, smell, and taste an elephant when the animal is quite dead. If he hears an elephant trumpeting or merely shuffling his feet, he had better watch out. Something is going on. Force is operating."[41]

So if revelation remains silent and visual, it loses personal force. It becomes mere information, dead with regard to its power to inspire reverence and personal presence. This explains why God was never content to do merely textual revelation. Every prophet was a speaking mouthpiece of God, not just a scribe. The Word made flesh wrote nothing, but spoke volumes. But since the Word of God today is preserved in literacy, the Bible itself also has bearing on how the Word of God is voiced in preaching and worship, and whether those voicings are more characterized by the dynamics of depersonalized literacy or personalizing orality.[42] Ong

---

40   Ibid., 112.

41   Ibid.

42   Stephen Webb calls this role of sound in worship "acoustemology" (*Divine Voice*, 27) and considers it a relatively unexplored phenomenon. Webb also coins the word "theo-acoustics" (chap. 2) to address the theological nature of sound and hearing, and references Ong as follows: "Only the sense of hearing can do justice to the way God is simultaneously with us and beyond us. Put another way, the voice of God reveals God's innermost purposes without exposing God to our objectifying gaze. Sound is the medium that best carries a supernatural message, because it delivers something external without putting us in control of its source. For Ong, hearing puts us in touch with another person in an immediate and inward way while, paradoxically, preserving some distance between us" (*Divine Voice*, 39–40).

believes these different voicings make a huge difference in terms
of revelatory presence: "As establishing personal presence, the word
has immediate religious significance, particularly in the Hebrew
and Christian tradition, where so much is made of a personal,
concerned God."[43]

Loss of Shared Experience

Since Ong names sound as the sense that most fosters unity,
a loss of Scripture as sound in the Christian community will
result in a loss of shared experience.[44] Better than sight, touch,
and smell, sound functionally pulls people together. Like smell,
it surrounds and penetrates and, more capably than sight, it can
carry language instead of mere print on page. Consider a slide
show of silent, language-free images. While they might still convey
an approximate message, it will necessarily lack the clarity and
warmth of an embodied voice looking us in the eye.[45]

Ong continues, "Encounters with others in which no words are
ever exchanged are hardly encounters at all. The written word
alone will not do, for it is not sufficiently living and refreshing."[46]
It is not enough for people to gather together in silence. Ong
requires sound to penetrate the silence. Here we start to see
why sermons as public addresses have such a long and persistent
role in the worship gathering. You would think that with all the
technology at our disposal, we really wouldn't still need the live
sermon. All the content of the sermon can be delivered with
other mediums. Yet we sense the need to still gather, to still honor
and make room for the sermon monologue. It's because when
we experience something "live" together, we feel bound to those

---

43   Ong, *Presence of the Word*, 113.

44   Ong describes how silence undermines the building of community: "Thus
     because of the very nature of sound as such, voice has a kind of primacy
     in the formation of true communities of men, groups of individuals
     constituted by shared awarenesses" (ibid., 124).

45   The importance of Ong's sense of "predication" will be explained more
     fully in the section below titled "Loss of Erupted Truth."

46   Ong, *Presence of the Word*, 125.

around us. It's the difference between a concert and a CD, a play in the theater and a DVD.

Loss of Simultaneity

Ong claims that sight comes to us in sequence, but sound comes all at once. Sight gives a slice of reality (since we can only see in one direction at a time), whereas sound comes to us in overwhelmingly simultaneous and uncontrollable ways. We can close our eyes, but we can't close our ears.[47] Sound comes whether we want it or not, making it the communicative medium that is the hardest to suppress and manage: "Of its very nature, the sound world has depth, dimension, fullness such as the visual, despite its own distinctive beauties, can never achieve."[48] A live speaker, of course, employs both the visual and the auditory senses. But even if an audience turns away, or is distracted from the face of the speaker, spoken words roll on in unavoidable ways, building an unrelenting sense of communicative force.

Loss of Erupted Truth

Ong is concerned not with the loss of truth in general, but the loss of truth erupting within time to a specific audience. This is abstract, but we've all felt it. For Ong, erupted truth occurs when a speaker not only thinks an opinion but voices it out into the room for others to hear.[49] There is a magic moment between a speaker and a hearer in real time. It's the natural impulse behind all live speech. It is the moment when the opinion is spoken and mutually perceived that propels a sense of a "live" grasp of a truth. This is what Ong calls "the moment of truth" and we quote him here at length:

---

47   As Ong says, "[T]here is no auditory equivalent to averting one's face or eyes" (ibid., 130).

48   Ibid.

49   Ong can't envision neutral speech. Speech always weighs in with personal force: "There is only one place in the intellective or knowledge process where the question of truth or falsity directly applies: this is the point at which we form a judgment, at which we predicate something of something, join a subject and a predicate" (ibid., 151).

What we have called the taste of truth appears to have no real duration. I possess the truth, savor it, test it, know it as truth and not falsity, in the judgment "This is an overcoat," not simply when the concepts represented by these words pass through my consciousness but more properly at the instant, the "moment of truth," when I *experience* the juncture of subject and predicate, the moment when (after sensing the meaning of the judgment, if you want, in advance), I actually taste its meaning, when the statement comes alive and flashes into consciousness so that I sense that it signifies, that is says something, so that I can "tell" it is true or false. This moment of truth is hard to pin down exactly. It is after I say "This" and probably before I quite finish "overcoat."[50]

To put it another way, our minds store all kinds of information about everything from history and pop culture to theological categories like sin and salvation. What we normally mean by "know" is that we can recall necessary facts. But this is far different from really knowing: "[I]n the strict sense we actually know to the full what we are actually 'judging' here and now for its truth or falsity."[51] Ong is saying nothing less than we know via speaking, and not just any kind of speaking but rather a "tasting" of words in a kind of intimate and mutual dialogue.[52]

Reading out loud, while a form of speaking, is entirely different. It is motivated not by a firsthand offer from speaker to audience, but

---

50 Ibid., 154.

51 Ibid.

52 Ong describes how speaking requires us to interact with ourselves: "Speaking and hearing are not simple operations. Each exhibits a dialectical structure which mirrors the mysterious depths of man's psyche. As he composes his thoughts in words, a speaker or writer hears this word echoing within himself and thereby follows his own thought, as though he was another person. Conversely, a hearer or reader repeats within himself the words he hears and thereby understands them, as though he were himself two individuals." Walter J. Ong, "Voice as Summons for Belief: Literature, Faith, and the Divided Self," *Thought* 33, no. 1 (1958), 51, quoted in *Ong Reader*, 261.

by reporting a prior idea. There is no composition going on, no flash of understanding, no eruption of truth from tongue. A reader may be a good reader but can never match the communicative intensity of an orator discovering out loud. This is why the more reliant a speaker is upon notes, the less true "knowing" is actually experienced by anyone in the room.

As preachers we've been commonly trained to write down all our thoughts in silence, and well before delivery, thereby unwittingly violating the very ways that discourse operates naturally between people. We don't jot down notes to say to our children before tucking them in at night.[53] To preach well, we need to be in a sort of discovery mode, which is categorically different than a reporting mode. These represent different genres of speech, each of which possesses distinct characteristics. A sermon in discovery mode is its own genre of speech, operating by its own rules of preparation and delivery.

Speech Genres

To flesh out the idea of a sermon in discovery mode it is helpful to consider what communication scholars call speech genres. The prominent theorist in speech genres is Russian linguist Mikhail Bakhtin. Bakhtin has, more than anyone since ancient times, reflected upon the nuances of interpersonal communication in a multifaceted world. We have different styles or genres for varying

---

53 If this connection between a sermon and bedtime chatter seems inappropriate, Mikhail Bakhtin (discussed in the next section) continually and repeatedly makes recourse to "everyday" communicative rejoinders as the sort of bedrock of organic relational competence. We have specific patterns in the way we greet, congratulate, and say farewell. These are unwritten rules that dictate how we respond to each other, and they extend into the ways we inquire about each other's health, family, and business. We don't start from scratch; we follow patterns we picked up very early in life. These patterns vary according to different contexts, and the sermon itself is a kind of speech pattern or genre. The chitchat in the lobby after the sermon is another kind. See M. M. Bakhtin, *Speech Genres and Other Late Essays*, ed. Caryl Emerson and Michael Holquist, trans. Vern W. McGee (1979; Austin: University of Texas Press, 1986), 77, 78, 79, 83, 89, 92, 94, 95, 96, 98, etc.

purposes and diverse environments. The unconscious rules for
a cell phone call are distinct from those for a wedding toast or a
board meeting. Speech genres work silently, behind the scenes as
they condition our expression. Bakhtin makes these observations:
"We speak only in definite speech genres, that is, all our utterances
have definite and relatively stable typical forms of construction of
the whole. Our repertoire of oral (and written) speech genres is
rich. We use them confidently and skillfully *in practice*, and it is
quite possible for us not even to suspect their existence *in theory*."[54]

Just as we brush our teeth according to certain unconscious
rhythmic/kinetic patterns, we communicate not randomly, but in
accordance with unwritten rules of each genre's expression.[55] We
learn to compose our actual speech organically, without conscious
effort. We mimic what we have experienced. As we preach we tend
to fall into sermonic patterns that imitate the genre of sermons we
have for years experienced. We move automatically, unconsciously
into "sermon" genre. Nobody has to announce it, it just happens.

But what if the sermons we have experienced and learned from
are what Bakhtin called "objectively neutral,"[56] composed and
delivered without regard to the others in the room? That would
make them deeply monological, independent of others. Any
sermon genre that separates the preacher and his thoughts from
the actual needs of the flock is deeply flawed. Bakhtin cannot
overstress how strongly a conscious sense of the audience can and
should impact a speech: "As we know, the role of the others for
whom the utterance is constructed is extremely great. We have

---

54 Ibid., 78.
55 Bakhtin observes how we have come to use language in our most natural
    and unforced settings: "We know our native language . . . not from
    dictionaries and grammars but from concrete utterances that we hear and
    that we ourselves reproduce in live speech communication with people
    around us" (ibid.).
56 For Bakhtin, the dangers of forgetting one's audience were potentially
    severe: "Objectively neutral styles presuppose something like an identity
    of the addressee and the speaker, a unity of their viewpoints, but this
    identity and unity are purchased at the price of almost complete forfeiture
    of expression" (ibid., 98).

already said that the role of these others, for whom my thought becomes actual thought for the first time (and thus also for my own self as well), is not that of passive listeners, but of active participants of speech communication."[57]

Notice how the crafting of words on another's behalf produces "actual thought for the first time" for both the speaker and the audience. This is the same sense of live oral composition that Ong has described where chosen words, while admittedly affected by prior preparation, are nevertheless specifically selected in that very moment for that exact set of listeners. This is why sermons that are read lose something vital. We have, for all intents and purposes, jettisoned the real others from the room.

In the discovery genre, the preacher is not relying upon precrafted words, but is actually choosing specific words for that moment and the audience senses the difference. This is what Ong has called a "flash" of understanding, and Bakhtin calls a "spark."[58] Sparks and flashes are not necessarily smooth: "We do not string together words smoothly and we do not proceed from word to word; rather, it is as though we fill in the whole with the necessary words."[59] In other words, live speech is messier and less polished than precrafted speech.

But I know what you're thinking. You can sense the value of live speech and discovery mode, but it seems incompatible with at least two pretty important homiletic features: preparation and authority. First, how could one "discover" things one already knows and has prepared? Second, would the emphasis on the audience, necessary for this genre, erode the sense of divine authority? Is not the message a word from God and not a mere product of the room and its people?

Preparation

Let's consider the first concern. Preparation is no enemy to the discovery genre. On the contrary, adequate preparation is absolutely

---

57   Ibid., 94.
58   Ibid., 87. See extract quotation of Ong earlier in the text of this chapter, cited at note 50.
59   Ibid., 86.

essential. Discovery mode should never be pitted against preparation since it requires good preparation to build steady and deep
understanding and the resulting natural fluency. The ideas themselves are well prepared, just not their specific or precise expression.
They are in memory, but at the beginning of the sermon, in a sort
of hibernation. The preacher then awakens those prepared ideas in
the timeliness of the moment.

This requires a confidence in the capacity of memory so that
the preacher, in time and space with the congregation, is able to
"discover" the truths that are, strictly speaking, already known.
That "discovery" animates the sermon and makes a shared
experience dialogue instead of monologue, unfolding instead of
finished, and eruptive rather than calculated.

Authority

This dialogical aspect also raises the question of authority. If it
is dialogue that is being produced, what is the precise relationship
between God, preacher, and audience? Does this weaken the
sermon's authority? Is God reduced to a conversation partner while
humans are inappropriately elevated to the role of co-composing
their own divine revelation?

This process need not and cannot compromise divine authority
in the sermon. It is God himself who graciously calls us to
dialogue. In the middle of a passage full of divine authority it is
God who invites: "'Come now, and let us reason together,' says
the LORD, 'Though your sins are as scarlet, they will be as white
as snow; though they are red like crimson, they will be like wool'"
(Isa. 1:18). The spoken word from God is a dialogue, but not
between equals.

Here we run into that mysterious overlap of word, preacher, and
people. A sermon has lines connecting all three parties in dialogue.
It is this sense of participatory dialogue that discovery fosters.
This is more risky since it precludes choosing all the right words
ahead of time, a safety net that creates precision but extinguishes

discovery and what Bakhtin calls "dialogical overtones."[60] These overtones are extinguished if the preacher already "knows" too much too soon and practically, if not technically, ignores the others in the room. There is no discovery left, nothing to move us off our previously composed script. This, says Ong, is the by-product of overdependence on the tools of literacy and an unwitting negligence of an earlier, more dynamic model of communication.

---

60   Bakhtin describes these higher tones as what gives speech communication a sense of dialogue, of give-and-take, and of responsiveness within what otherwise appears to be a mere monologue (*Speech Genres and Other Late Essays*, 92). For Bakhtin a sermon should recognize not just the present audience, but the entire older and longer conversation to which the sermon is responding. No sermon starts from scratch, even as it is bound to a previously delivered scriptural text. For an analysis of Bakhtin's sense of dialogical overtones in Scripture itself, see Walter L. Reed's *Dialogues of the Word: The Bible as Literature according to Bakhtin* (Oxford: Oxford University Press, 1993).

7

FINDING THE SERMON THAT'S "ALREADY THERE"

*Then Moses said to the LORD, "Please, Lord, I have never
been eloquent, neither recently nor in time past, nor since You have
spoken to Your servant; for I am slow of speech and slow of tongue."
The LORD said to him, "Who has made man's mouth? Or who makes
him mute or deaf, or seeing or blind? Is it not I, the LORD?
Now then go, and I, even I, will be with your mouth,
and teach you what you are to say."*

Exodus 4:10–12

In 1987, I was a student in seminary. The church where I
interned allowed me one of my first chances to preach. My
topic that day was "The Friendless American Male." It was a
topic borrowed from pop sociology, and I thought it was a good
introduction to the book of 1 Samuel.

So I preached about the friendship of David and Jonathan. I
distilled some practical tips for being a good friend. It seemed like
a winner all around: culturally sensitive and biblically based. By
God's providence, my homiletics professor was in the audience that
day. You remember preaching labs—those videotaped chambers
where we all gave our best shot to a small audience of our peers
and had to view the results later and write an accompanying self-
evaluation essay. That was not my idea of real preaching.

Finding the Sermon in the Text

But that morning I was excited to have a live audience, a real room, and a trendy topic. I thought I did a decent job. While no revival broke out, I was quite sure several friendships were saved that day. So I was looking forward to hearing what my instructor would say in feedback. His words, which I still remember twenty-seven years later, were charitable, but blunt. "It was a pretty good sermon," he said, my confidence rising. "Except for one thing. Everything you said was true. It just isn't in 1 Samuel." The words, gently spoken, hit like a two-by-four. What? Not in 1 Samuel? But I referenced a dozen different verses!

That was early in my education. I hadn't yet been taught how to respectfully listen to the text. I hadn't learned how to find the author's intent. From what I had seen and heard, Scripture was there for the taking. It could be pulled out and applied to any subject, just add in the verses. Gradually I came to learn a more respectful approach. I remember lightbulbs coming on in a later class I took on preaching biblical narrative. We were shown how the given chapter doesn't mean just anything or everything. It means something. We have to look for it, for what the author had in mind. A sort of adventure opened up in hermeneutics. Though it may sound obvious, I had to learn that Scripture is not a grab bag for pulling out whatever you need for the sermon. It comes to us with a specific message embedded in it. I had no idea that within each text of Scripture, a sermon already lies latent, waiting to be drawn out again.

Preachers of the Book

Anyone signing up to become a preacher is tied to the text. We preachers differ from other public speakers in our reliance upon the sacred text of Scripture. While politicians and lawyers may make reference to legal code, they are not faced with the preacher's task of actually representing an ancient text to a contemporary audience. This is one of the reasons that preaching retains such a strong connection to literacy. Without Scripture, there would be no authoritative preaching, only the opinions of one person against another.

But there's a danger when preachers approach the pulpit with two texts: the text of Scripture and the text of their own notes. Though related, priority seems to be given to the notes most recently penned or printed, and preachers may, in terms of what is granted the most attention, focus more on their own "text." This is what I was doing in my previously mentioned sermon. Without meaning to, I put Scripture in a subservient role so that the essence of my message, while touching on Scripture, was actually propelled more from my own notes. The flow of thought in the sacred text was sacrificed to the needs of my outline and a connection to cultural relevance.

In oral preaching, the sacred text is approached differently. There is only one authoritative text, and that text is binding upon preacher and congregation. The preachers' task, clearly, is to orally animate a text that is not their own. There is only one authority. The oral sermon is more likely to follow the flow of thought actually in the passage and not to construct separate outlines.

This is where scriptural context becomes important. If the sermon is to reflect the biblical author's original thought, that thought has to be pulled from the context of the entire book. If it is John's or Isaiah's message, the preacher needs to understand John and Isaiah in context. They must "hear" and hear well this ancient author.[1] This is why it is important to preach with sensitivity to broad scriptural context and almost always directly through an entire book. The sermon's structure has to respect the flow of thought in the source text instead of inventing an entirely new structure. Of course, these are generalities. It is possible to preach topically in an oral style and to preach through a book in a literary style. But there is a natural connection between an oral approach and preaching all the way through a book.

---

1   Augustine assumes the preacher's aim is to recover the intent of the original author (see *De doctrina christiana* 1.37.41).

The Great Relief

When we actually submit to the original author's flow of thought, preaching is then not the complex thing we've been taught it was. Crafting our own separate structure out of the text can consume an enormous percentage of our available hours in preparation. It's possible to spend as much as 90 percent of this time building some sort of literary framework to carry the central message. When the outline is done, the sermon is ready.

Oral preaching allocates the hours differently. While we might spend the same total time in preparation, the scale tips away from entirely literary preparation and moves it toward the tasks of oral preparation. That topic will be covered in detail in the next chapter. Right now the point is simply this: it's possible to abandon entirely the notion that we have to create a sermon each week. We don't have to create anything. There's already a sermon written for us each week. The sermon is the scriptural text. That text is enough. Let's not spend our time creating a second text to clarify the first text.

This is a shift away from almost every contemporary model. You know how it normally goes: (1) study the text, (2) establish the central meaning in the original historical context, (3) distill that meaning down to a central premise, (4) find or create a structure for that premise (which will become your outline, your flow of thought), and (5) sprinkle in supporting material to illustrate and apply the central premise and supporting points.

Preachers spend an awful lot of time at step 4. Homiletic textbooks give us all sorts of ideas for structuring our thoughts. Once we have our central premise, we're told we need to find a vehicle to carry and organize our thoughts. Without it, we'll just ramble around in the pulpit. So structures, which by the way can also be found in any public speaking textbook, can take many forms. We can structure our sermons as problem/solution or as cause/effect. If you choose the first, you'll spend the first half of your sermon laying out the problem that is underlying your text. You'll spend the latter half of your sermon laying out the solutions.

Each half will probably have a couple points and subpoints. You can imagine how it would work with cause/effect. Those are only two examples.

You can adopt a chronological structure where you are tracing the history of something. You can have topical structure where you're breaking a thing down into its component parts. You can use an order of inquiry where you describe the steps you took to come to a conclusion. You can have an elimination order (not this, not this, not this, but this) or a spatial structure where you proceed from far away to near, from east to west, or from heaven to earth. You get the idea. Depending on the textbook you consult, it's not hard to find a dozen or more organizational patterns to choose from.[2]

In reading this you might naturally feel a twinge of guilt and think, "Uh-oh. I think I use the same pattern all the time. I forgot there were so many." We do tend to get stuck in a certain pattern of thinking, and it's healthy to survey other ways to handle a central premise. Certainly the impulse to lend a sense of order and progression to a sermon is commendable. But remember these techniques come from the world of communication in general where the speaker is saddled with the job of inventing all the content.[3] In that position, you need a structure, and you must fabricate your own.

But this is not our situation. We have this book, this already-delivered text. The text already has a flow of thought. What if—and this is the radical proposal—we simply followed that structure for our sermon? What if we simply reanimated the original

---

2   One of my favorite patterns of organization is one invented by Eugene Lowry in *The Homiletical Plot: The Sermon as Narrative Art Form*, rev. ed. (Louisville: Westminster John Knox, 2001). He shows how any sermon can follow the same sequence of upsetting equilibrium and introducing really good news to a dire situation.

3   "Inventing" is the correct term here both practically and technically. Invention is the first stage in classical rhetorical theory. Choosing your structure is part of this stage and the stage that follows, which is arrangement.

author's flow of thought and called that our sermon? So the order would go like this: (1) study the text, (2) internalize the author's flow of thought, and (3) reproduce that flow of thought for your specific setting. That's it.

This might raise some objections. For instance, the original flow of thought is too vague and meandering for the contemporary mind or maybe too simplistic. Perhaps people need a clearer, more organized version. But can we really improve on Moses' or Paul's flow of thought? Does it not come to us in the way it is for a purpose? Must we really adopt an editor's role and clean it up with some good contemporary word structure?

If sermons were essays, that would be one thing. If sermons are required to have literary coherence, then they need a suitable structure. But if sermons were allowed to run by different rules, by what we saw described in chapter 6 as the psychodynamics of orality, then maybe the author's flow of thought is good enough. If so, we have simplified our task considerably. We bind ourselves to the text, not just in its conclusions or implications, but in how the Holy Spirit tumbled it out of the author's mouth and eventual pen. What a relief to think of the sermon as "already there."

I'm currently preaching through Isaiah. I usually have a chapter, sometimes two, in consideration each week. That's the portion of text I have to assimilate, wrestle with, and internalize from Isaiah's book for Sunday. But I don't have to create a sermon. It's as if I'm saying to Isaiah, "Hey, it's me. I'm way down here twenty-seven centuries after you. I'm trying to follow you, to hear you, to 'get' you. You're in charge here. I'm just following your lead. Not that I fully grasp what you're saying. You confuse me a lot. And you repeat yourself so much. So much geography. But my job is not to explain you. My job is not to demystify you or defang you or tone you down. I believe your sermon is the one my flock needs to hear. I wish you could be here to do it yourself. But you're not. So I'm going to stand in your stead. And I'm going to try, as best I can, to preach your sermon. I'm not original, and thank God I don't have to be. God, help me preach Isaiah's sermon."

The Pain

An oral approach to preaching does bring relief, but also a painful reality. So let's talk about the pain. If we commit to preaching other people's sermons (those of the biblical authors), we have decided to bind ourselves to context. I can't follow Isaiah's flow in one chapter if I'm not "getting" him as a person and a preacher. How do I do that? Well if Isaiah's order means anything, it means it comes to us with some sequence in flow, not just in a given chapter, but in the book as a whole.[4] For me, that means that all the chapters before chapter 30 will help me uncover the sermon in chapter 30. For me, that means I'm going to preach them in order. So here comes the pain. Isaiah has sixty-six chapters. You might be thinking, "There's no way in the world I can preach sixty-six chapters in a row."

Nowadays only a minority of preachers are preaching their way through a whole book of the Bible. It's out of step. It's not what most churches are doing. But we're not exploring what's most practical or what works. We're talking about our role as preachers bound to a Book. Can we really say we're bound to a Book that we use more as a springboard to cultural issues? Can we really say we're bound to a Book whose content we pull out, reorganize, and restructure for relevance?

Now in actuality, I'm not taking sixty-six weeks to get through Isaiah. I'm taking a total of forty-four weeks along with a five-week break in the middle for a topical series. So the longest we'll be in Isaiah without a break is about twenty-five weeks at a time. Still a long time by today's standards. We're only halfway through. But I can tell you I'm just starting to "get" Isaiah. I've never felt more energized in preaching. The continuity of the series, the healthy sense of repetition, and Isaiah's unrelenting drive toward exposing shallow faith are all exactly what our people need. So it hasn't been that painful.

---

4   I'm aware of all the theories about Isaiah's composition and that it didn't all come at the same time and place. But I think each book, as we have received it, still holds together as a unit. This is my assumption when I consider any book in its current form.

One serendipitous benefit is that when you do this, you have many weeks mapped out in advance. You and your flock always know where you're going, at least in the sense of which chapter will arrive when. For Isaiah we even printed out little bookmarks with the schedule for the book printed right on it. We ask people to put it in their Bibles and read along for the whole series. When we come to something touchy, where Isaiah makes a poignant or controversial implication, everybody knows I didn't plan it that way. I didn't concoct a schedule or choose a text to give me permission to say something blunt. The sense is that God has timed the series and each week we look forward to what Isaiah has for us. The pressure is on Isaiah, not me. We have found it timely, the way things come to us. We are letting God speak. We don't feel in charge of the process. Isn't that how it's supposed to be?

Although I'm not selling this approach on practicality, I do have to highlight another practical benefit. When you bounce around to a different book of the Bible each week, you spend a lot of time in extra backgrounding. If you're going to be responsible, you have to review a new historical setting with each passage. New cultural and geographic issues. Since you have to try to place your text in the context of the larger book, you have to read the passages on both sides of your selected text. All this requires extra time in research. In contrast, when you stay in a book from start to finish, all those issues remain steady from week to week. The historical context might evolve, but it does so gradually. The work I did in background study for Isaiah bears fruit for forty-four weeks, not just one.

There's a way to preach even long books and treat them as a cohesive unit. Only Psalms is longer than Isaiah by chapters. And the Psalms are structurally broken into five subbooks. Make a separate series out of each subbook. Maybe you want to move faster through some books or treat some sections in an overview. I preached the Minor Prophets once by handling one prophet each week. There are ways to do this creatively. In the end, we just have to decide if we're willing to let the Book be the Book, or whether we're in charge of the Book. It's submitting to the text as is, believing that God put it that way for a purpose.

8

SWALLOWING THE WORD

Building a Sermon Inside You

Then He said to me, "Son of man, eat what you find; eat this scroll,
and go, speak to the house of Israel." So I opened my mouth, and He
fed me this scroll. He said to me, "Son of man, feed your stomach and
fill your body with this scroll which I am giving you." Then I ate it,
and it was sweet as honey in my mouth.

Ezekiel 3:1–3

From where I lived in Akron, Ohio, it's about a two-hour drive to Pittsburgh. I was doing it twice a week for my doctoral program. Two hours there, two hours back. Eight hours a week on the road. I learned every conceivable way to get between those two points. Interstates, back roads, everything along that spectrum. Every combination of any possible route. I always had an inner urge to find a faster, more efficient, way. Behind it was the magical thinking that there existed somewhere a sort of Northwest Passage or wormhole through which a person could, by the sheer novelty of discovery, shave twenty minutes off the trip. But alas, it always took two hours no matter how hard I tried.

At the time I was a working as a full-time pastor and preaching regularly. So I always had a sermon in the pipeline. I tried to redeem the time by working on my sermon as I drove. I often listened to an audio recording of the text.[1] And while listening I would have ideas. Things I wanted to jot down. Things I wanted to fit into the sermon. But I was driving. It wasn't practical to pull over to make note of something. I'd be late to class.

A Surprising Thing I Learned While Driving

Then very naturally and without a lot of conscious thought, I began to try something new. I started keeping a mental log of things I wanted to put in the sermon. It was something I could do while driving. I would think to myself, "That reminds me of the Band-Aid principle." And I would make a place in my mind to hold that thought. But before I knew where to hold it, I had to ask myself, "Where do you want to put that? In the introduction? No. Later. In the conclusion. That could be my conclusion or application." So I would mentally put it later, toward the end. I visualized it at the bottom of a blank "screen." That left empty space up above that I could mentally fill with additional elements.

At first it was tough because I had the natural impulse to want to write everything down. It's that fear we have that if we don't note it, we'll lose it. That's why when you wake up in the night remembering something you have to do, you have to jot it down before you can relax and go back to sleep. Nurtured as we are in literacy, we don't have any idea how much capacity for memory and organization God built into us.

But the more I did the mental log thing, the better I got. I started to organize a number of things in my head and keep them in a sequential order. I had to, because I was determined to make use of the time and I didn't want to pull over. Little did I know God was showing me something about how he designed us. About that same time I was discovering Walter Ong. Ong started to make sense of this for me. He started to show me that before

---

1   Technology continues to give us newer ways to convert text to sound. When I first started doing this I used a cassette tape of the Bible, which eventually gave way to a CD. Now I use both web-based audio versions in various translations and my smartphone onto which I've recorded myself reading the chapter using a voice memo app.

writing came along and took over everything, people had extensive ability to speak from memory. I'm not talking about memorization. That's something else—a word-for-word parroting. I started to see that memory is different. It's an ability to tell a story and just know what comes next. It's the ability to put things in the kind of order in which one thing leads to the next. And we all have this ability. But our dependency on literacy shrank this capacity just as surely as the calculator destroyed our natural capacity for doing math in our head. If you don't have to use memory, you won't. If you don't, your memory muscle atrophies and you become convinced you can't keep anything in your head.

So imagine my excitement when Ong started showing me the historical grounding for what I was simultaneously attempting to do just out of necessity. No wonder there's a picture of Ong hanging in my office. It was a rare privilege to stumble onto a scholar who puts things in place for you. The kind of mentor who articulates things you've been wrestling with and keeps flipping on lightbulb after lightbulb until you are able to see things clearly and in a new way. Ong helped me to see the possibility of building a sermon from the inside out. And he pointed me in directions that showed me how old and how theologically grounded this practice has always been. This used to be the common way it was done. And it all starts with allowing Scripture to penetrate us from the inside out.

Internalization of Scripture

Let's start with our familiarity with Scripture. Just as sermons can remain "outside" us in notes or on a screen, the Word of God can similarly remain outside us if we only refer to it in text. Scripture itself gives the example of a prophet eating a scroll as the Word of God, internalized.[2] Jesus framed the Word of God as essential food to be taken in (Matt. 4:4), as did Moses before him (Deut. 8:3).[3]

---

2   See Ezekiel 2:8–3:4; see also Jeremiah 15:16; Revelation 10:9–10; cf. 1 Timothy 4:15.

3   Related to taking in God's Word as food, see various passages about

When we read any of Augustine's sermons and attempt to count the number of scriptural references, it immediately becomes clear that Augustine had so much Scripture internalized that it came out in all sorts of quotes, references, and even subtle allusions. At times it is hard to decipher where Augustine's words stop and Scripture begins. This is not because Augustine memorized the sermon. He internalized the Scripture that then leaked extemporaneously into the sermon.[4] This ability to recall things organically, common in the ancient world, has all but disappeared in our post–printing press world.

You've probably sensed the difference in your audience's response when you quote Scripture right in the middle of a sermon. There is a qualitative, more authoritative sound. The congregation can sense it and so can you. Unfortunately, most of us don't have a large reservoir of internalized Scripture to draw upon. This has multiple causes, not the least of which is the lazy memory produced by access to so much print. Why should we memorize anything we can easily look up?

Adding to the problem is so many new translations of the Bible. For better or for worse, when one standard English version was established, all ears became tuned to that familiar vocabulary. Now no one knows what Scripture "should" sound like because we all hear it in so many different versions and with increasing levels of paraphrasing. But if Walter Ong is right about the theology of sound, we must find a way to release Scripture into a room. Whether in oral readings, oral interpretation of Scripture, scriptural songs, or Scripture embedded in sermons, it must rise off

---

meditating on Scripture such as the Lord's admonitions to Joshua (Josh. 1:8), the psalmist's description of the righteous (Ps. 1:2–3), and Paul's exhortation to the believers in Colossae (Col. 3:16). All of this sustained thinking and reflecting on the text serves to help us internalize what God has said in the Bible.

4   Schaeffer further explains how engaged a preacher must be with the written Word: "If the preacher is to rhapsodize on a topic, drawing from a copia informed by the reading of scripture, then scripture and its wisdom are obviously not outside the speaker, but interiorized" ("Dialectic of Orality and Literacy," 1139).

the silent page, into our hearts and minds and out of our mouths. It must become internal so that it can become naturally external.

But here a motive check is in order. Remember, Augustine didn't memorize all that Scripture to be a better preacher. He would have done it if he never preached another sermon. He did it for its own value, as discussed in chapter 2. It just so happens that when Scripture is internalized (whether in exact wording or just in clear meaning), God can use that resource in a sermon, perhaps even in ways we can't and shouldn't plan.

This makes us rethink the entire relationship of Scripture to the sermon. If we think of the sermon as the primary outcome of the passage, then a good deal of our week will be focused on that end: the production of a sermon. The Scripture becomes a means to an end. This sets us up to "use" Scripture and to keep Scripture in a very functional, pragmatic role—in a place that is subservient to the sermon.

But what if Scripture was the preacher's stimulus to God and people all week long? The week's passage would then not be detached from the rest of life and reserved exclusively for the sermon. It would have a much broader saturation into the preacher's life. It would first function as the preacher's fuel for the week both devotionally and then in every meeting and interaction. Indeed, it would then be almost impossible to calculate how much time was spent on sermon preparation because the interiorization of the passage would become more a way of thinking that week than a project to be completed. This is what the ancient oral way suggests to us: the sermon as the overflow of a saturated life, a life marinated in Scripture and in this week's passage. It is the love of God and his Word in a nonpragmatic sense that is the foundation of oral preaching.

This might seem like a tall order with today's busy schedules. Sometimes we just want to get through our long task list, get to all our meetings, manage people well, and somehow find time to squeeze out an additional fifteen hours or more in sermon preparation. But often those fifteen hours are in a separate world from the rest of life, and the week's passage is confined to the office or where we study at home. Though heavily scrutinized, exposed, and outlined for content, the text doesn't leak much into the rest of the preacher's world. And we wonder why we struggle, at the end of our long study, to find good points of application to life. So if we were to operate differently in relation to our sermon text, how would it look in everyday life?

The Devotional Role of the Passage

In the ancient world, orators spent a lot of time in what they called "status" contemplation. This is where we just sit with a text to determine its place, or status, in the world and the world of ideas. It's not a stage where we're building anything, but merely a time for asking questions.[5] Quintilian's outline of status theory (*Institutio oratoria* 3.9.6) during preparation has direct application to the way a sermon is approached. Typically we move from hermeneutics to homiletics with too much haste. Once we think we understand the gist of a text, we want to start composing the sermon. "Let's get going," we say to ourselves. "We only have so much time." But status theory asks us to dissect the idea first. Grasp it from the ground up. Get the "why" before the "what." Make the personal application to your heart and life.

Take, for instance, Jesus' exhortation at the end of the Sermon on the Mount to be "perfect" or, perhaps, "complete." Before we jump to composing a sermon on that, we must ask: what does he mean by complete? We ask that of ourselves, but we also invite God into the reflection. We ask him to show us. What is the opposite of complete? What would keep a person incomplete?

---

5   We can see the exhaustive nature of Quintilian's inquiry into any subject in the following quote: "To sum up the whole in a few words, then, arguments are drawn from persons, causes, places, time (of which we distinguished three parts: the preceding, the coincident, and the subsequent), manner (that is, how a thing has been done), means (under which we included instruments), definition, genus, species, differences, peculiarities, removal, division, beginning, increase, completion, similarity, dissimilarity, contraries, consequences, causes, effects, issues, connection, and comparison, each of which is divided into several species" (*Institutio oratoria* 5.10.94).

To what extent am I, the preacher, complete? How would I know if I was complete? Does he say how to become complete? What are the implications of being complete? Or of being incomplete? What are the obstacles? What hazards? What rewards or benefits? How would I recognize it in others? How would others recognize it in me? What other terms might people use to describe it? Why do we persist in remaining immature or incomplete? Does completion mean sinless perfection? If not, how is it different? What are counterfeits of completion? What confusions does the concept arouse? What does culture at large think of completion? Buddhists? Pagans? Old people? Young? Why did Jesus conclude his sermon with that command?

This is a sample of the kinds of questions that can be contemplated in status. Asking questions creates tension, which nudges us forward on our quest of seeking to better understand. The goal is to gain a devotional curiosity about the subject that is connected to our own lives and the lives of others. Curiosity is a kind of appetite or desire to learn, and such desires drive everything we do. So as we become curious and more interested in the text, we start to see the central issue of the passage show up in life. This produces a mental and verbal comfort level with every aspect of the text so that vital connections are made between the idea and actual lived experience. We discover why this idea needs to be preached, and why the original author was so worked up about it. After all, why did God put this here?

But the preacher concerned with efficiency will view that list of questions as daunting. Why dig into all that when there is no time to cover all that in the sermon? Well, one reason is because we should not be in the business of mouthing admonitions about real-ities we ourselves have never really understood at a gut level. We're trying to become better people. We're trying to acquire a love for truth, not just its expression. This kind of "deep" understanding will fuel a kind of grounded speaking that can sustain a live con-nection between mind and mouth, demonstrate credible ethos, and adapt to the moment. Admittedly, it's not instrumental toward merely producing a sermon. It's about understanding our Father's world and how he moves in it. Our curiosity must start and dwell there even if there are no obvious connections to the sermon.

There are no shortcuts—no cutting and pasting. We must start to feel at home with the passage at an elemental level with all the appropriate connections to anthropology, soteriology, and ecclesiology. The Word of God must rise up and capture us, so we can speak about it before it becomes a sermon, and the next week after the sermon is over. We can't just grab a truth, preach, and forget.

Well, we can. Sometimes we do. When we do, it's like the text sits on the outside, but never works its way in. Maybe we're in too much of a hurry. All this takes time. How much time should we give it? As much as is needed. It's the stage of preparation that's the most tempting to skip or shortchange because it doesn't feel "practical." We just want to make progress toward the goal. We want to have a sermon in our hands so we feel ready. But it's the most fruitful stage for producing the "good man" that the ancients believed was prior to the message. Without that good man, the sermon remains only theoretically true ideas assembled onto a page.

The Discipling Role of the Passage

The next stage of preparation utilizes another concept from the ancient world: dialogue. Having partners in dialogue is hardly a new idea, nor even an exclusive product of an oral orientation. Many homileticians have advised it as a helpful tool. Yet the most commonly understood use of dialogue is still very pragmatic. It envisions a group of people gathered to discuss a passage with the explicit goal of sermon production. Behind this advice is the commonsense notion that two or three or four heads are better than one. More minds thinking through the interpretive issues of a particular passage can provide greater understanding both in terms of the meaning of the text and the implications for that text upon real souls. On top of that, the brainstorming is just plain fun, especially over lunch. I've been in these kinds of sermon discussion groups, and they definitely do help me get a better grasp of the passage. But there is a danger here.

Just like we can "use" Scripture as a means to an end, we can also use people the same way. They become not our flock or colleagues, but our sermon helpers. Now some of them might even enjoy that role and not mind being used that way. But the dialogue itself must be inherently valuable. If we use them for a utilitarian end, something begins to break down. The problem with overt "sermon discussion" groups is their disproportionate elevation of the actual sermon. It is this remote event on Sunday that becomes the reason for meeting. It elevates the preacher above the others in a subtle way. Those discussions often remain cognitive and impersonal. It's relatively easy to discuss the passage, but harder to get around to the passage in our lives. Plus, only a handful of people will ever be motivated to meet and discuss a sermon.

But what if we moved more organically from the devotional stage to a conversational stage with whomever we encounter in a given week. This is not shoehorning it into our lives in a disciplined way. We naturally want to talk about what is life-giving, what is transforming. Since the passage is actually making us think differently . . . since it is becoming something internal, it springs to mind in the counseling session, in the meeting with the children's ministry team, and in the hospital visit. We can't help but bring it up. It's affecting our way of being in the world. We may not even be thinking of the sermon at this point. It's just popping up all the time because it's alive in us, and vital. We find ourselves talking about the passage in unforced ways in the normal rhythm of pastoral life.

As we speak about a passage with people close to us, we also allow their ideas to shape ours.[6] Our understanding of the text grows naturally. Especially if a congregation is going through an entire book together, that book becomes the functioning theme of the church. People are experiencing the book everywhere: in their own devotional reading, in their small groups, in casual lunch conversations. It builds community life and simplifies the focus of the flock. In all our ways of getting together, we are too

---

6   Quintilian holds up frequent discourse on all kinds of topics as the best form of general preparation (*Institutio oratoria* 2.2.5).

often studying two or three separate passages in the same week. How can we ever live out that much content? But if we are all focused on Mark or Philippians, or Isaiah together, we find common ground and common applications. This word from God is breaking out of the walls of the sermon. It becomes the basis for grounded community life and ministry together.

It just so happens that as we do this, it ends up helping us on Sunday too. We come to discover what we mean as we begin to speak it. As we hear ourselves and others speak, a connection starts to develop between mind and mouth, and fluency on the topic starts steadily rising. In terms of the sermon, the key here is verbal activity early in the week, long before Sunday arrives. But it's bigger and broader than that. It is the discipling role of Scripture within a congregation that goes on before, during, and after the sermon.

Developing a Conversational Tone

When the passage is first devotional and then discussed in meetings throughout the week, a conversational tone also makes its way into the actual sermon. I don't mean here turning the sermon into an actual large group discussion as some have argued.[7] Jesus spoke authoritatively without apology and used a lot of monologues. The apostles, though interactive in some contexts, also never shrank from extended monologues. Church history with its volumes of collected sermons suggests that sermons have been predominantly monological since Pentecost. But the audience can still be highly influential in the crafting and progression of the speech.[8]

---

7   Some recent homileticians have decided this dialogue can be literal and have called for the conversion of sermon from monologue to "multilogue." They picture the preacher as a sort of host or facilitator among multiple voices, calling out and addressing questions in a live discussion format. They see the monologue sermon often driven by power and illegitimate authority and are seeking a more democratic alternative.

8   Quintilian observes how an engaged audience actually encourages a speaker to adapt and be flexible: "For we are not as yet admitted to full

It's possible to have a conversational tone within the sermon even though it's a monologue. This is the basic task of persuasion. If we are attempting to persuade at any level, there must be an imagined audience to persuade. In that sense we must imagine and anticipate the audience's possible reactions to the point under discussion. There is the preacher on one side, and the congregation serving as a discussion partner on the other. So it is natural to use a conversational tone with statements like, "Now I know some of you are thinking . . ." or "Now here's the problem with what I just said." As we mention the natural objections or reservations that might reside in the audience, we not only bolster our case, but we achieve a sense of mutuality and the discovery mode established in chapter 6. Instead of talking at people, we are talking with them.

Roadmapping: The Natural Way to Remember What Comes Next

Although this chapter is about building a sermon, we've so far done little toward building anything we can point to as a sermon. It's been all about personal grounding and respect for the ways a passage works outside of Sunday. But something is being built, an essential capacity to preach in a more oral style. With that as a foundation, how do we proceed? What's the next stage for an oral preacher?

In many senses the background research a preacher does about a passage is no different in the oral model. We still have to do the work in translation, history and geography, and the consulting of commentaries. That work must typically happen in personal study, and that doesn't change. It's after that work is done that the difference begins to emerge. In most models, the fruit of research moves toward some sort of central premise, which is then structured into some kind of outline. Outlines maintain a monopoly in the homiletic world. Sermons can be pressured to

---

freedom of speech, and the attention of the audience, being still fresh, keeps us under restraint, but when their minds are propitiated and warmed, greater liberty will be tolerated" (*Institutio oratoria* 4.1.57).

squeeze into them. Outlines do not necessarily kill a sermon, but they're not the only way to organize content.

It's important, in an oral framing of content, to keep sequence or progression in mind. Outlines don't necessarily do this. If an outline has four reasons to persevere in suffering, and reasons 1 and 3 can be flipped without affecting anything, then there is no narrative structure to the content. It is organized more rationally and less in a necessary progression from one idea that leads to the next.[9] Building a structure block by block might be a better visual metaphor. The points of a sermon cannot be thrown out in random order.

Storytelling (whether around a campfire or in a sermon) is a genre where sequence is crucial, and sermons can be organized as unfolding stories even when the passage being preached is not itself a biblical story. In fact a narrative structure is central to an oral sermon as a way to keep hold of multiple ideas without forgetting what comes next. Most of us can retell a compelling story, even a long one, by memory even as we feel convinced we could never preach that long without an outline in front of us. But if the sermon were just a long story, episodic in structure—who knows how much we might be able to keep in mind?

Particularly pertinent is Quintilian's metaphor of the message as a journey and the various moves or structures of a message like different points on the map. With this orientation, the preacher (as traveler) is able to see the entire journey (*theoria*) even as individual stops are being singled out.[10]

In actual homiletic practice the road map can be drawn on paper or screen just like an outline. But instead of words, the map is entirely pictographic allowing us to keep five or six different "stops" along the journey clearly in mind (without memorizing anything in specific). In this sense, we can draw each "block" of

---

9   This is what Ong calls a narrative "story line" with "episodic" structure (*Orality and Literacy*, 138). If you're familiar with narrative structure in a sermon, this is the basic impulse.

10   Quintilian's term for this viewpoint or "place to see everything" is the Greek *theoria* (*Institutio oratoria* 10.7.14–16).

the sermon (which can be a story, illustration, quote, application, explanation of the text, photograph, or prop) on the sermon map. We can even include potential detours and optional routes. Sometimes we might not decide how to end a sermon until we're nearing the end. But if we have two possible options, there is flexibility.

A map maintains the organizing power of an outline, adds the sequencing of narrative structure, and employs the visual power pictures. With a little practice, we can actually visualize the sequence of the sermon on one page much faster than we could artificially memorize the numbered points and subpoints of an outline.[11] This tool or habit plumbs the vast powers of memory that have atrophied through centuries of textual laziness. The oral ancients saw memory (not memorization) as a powerful tool in speech.

How do we know what to actually start placing on our road map? Well we've already established that we're not trying to create a sermon, but to unleash the one that's already there in the text, which is becoming internalized in the preacher, and is permeating the lives of the congregation. So that helps a lot. At this point, we need to capture the original author's flow of thought by identifying and naming those "moves" that are key. In most sections that we'll preach, there won't be more than three to five significant moves or what we have come to call points. I like "moves"[12] better because it suggests a spatial progression from one place to the next. Once those are laid out, the road map is well on its way.

But it's important to note that not everything Isaiah or Paul says in a chapter is going to be on our road map. We have to try

---

11 Clyde Fant attempts something similar with his oral "sermon brief," which contains textual summaries of thought "blocks" and key transitioning sentences. See Clyde E. Fant, *Preaching for Today* (New York: Harper & Row, 1975), 170. Fant's sermon brief, however, looks suspiciously like an outline, and most new users would consider the difference hairsplitting. The innovation of the roadmap is the visual and iconic sense to the thought blocks that portrays a sense of destination toward a specific end, and the resultant ease of transfer to memory.

12 It was David Buttrick who first coined this phrase in narrative preaching. See David Buttrick, *Homiletic: Moves and Structures* (Philadelphia: Fortress, 1987).

to capture the general progression. But we can't get every detail. There is a selectiveness here, a filtering. The moves that make our road map are going to be major points of stress that we sense are most important to Isaiah or Paul. For instance, in a sermon on Isaiah 30, I might distill the content down to four moves: *Rebellion*, *Self-sufficiency*, *Discipline*, and *Restoration*. I don't concoct that flow. That's pretty much Isaiah's flow. I just listen to him until I hear where he is going.

Now at this point, I have to distill down which portions of my chapter I'm going to actually read out loud. I've learned that reading more than a verse at a time puts my eyes down and away from the congregation too long. Yet I need to point them to verses to establish where I'm drawing this idea. Since I only have these four moves, I'll need to make sure I draw out their corresponding verses. Those verses I will read out loud and stress. Other portions of this text I will need to paraphrase, and some I'll just skip. I know that sounds careless, but I'm usually covering a whole chapter each week. I have to focus in a few spots and summarize the rest. For the oral preacher, the whole story is more important than every detail. I've learned that by taking a chapter a week, I am more likely to balance both the forest and trees.

Once those moves and their verses are on the map, arranged in order, I have to think about ways to illustrate or apply them. So on my road map, I can either write the keyword *Rebellion* or have an illustration that captures rebellion. Let's say it's an illustration about a time when I didn't want to admit I was wrong about what time zone we were in. I might draw a little clock on my road map. Just a corny little clock. It doesn't mean anything to anyone else and it doesn't have to. That little clock symbolizes my rebellion and my rebellion is tied to the Israelites' stubbornness and rebellion. Just the visual icon is enough to remind me of that move.

So then I move on to *Self-sufficiency*. I think of how I'll explain that both in the ancient world and today. I'll think of another little icon (earplugs which represent tuning others out) and add it to my visual road map in the right sequence. So when I'm done I'll have four major moves in my sermon. I'll see how they're all connected

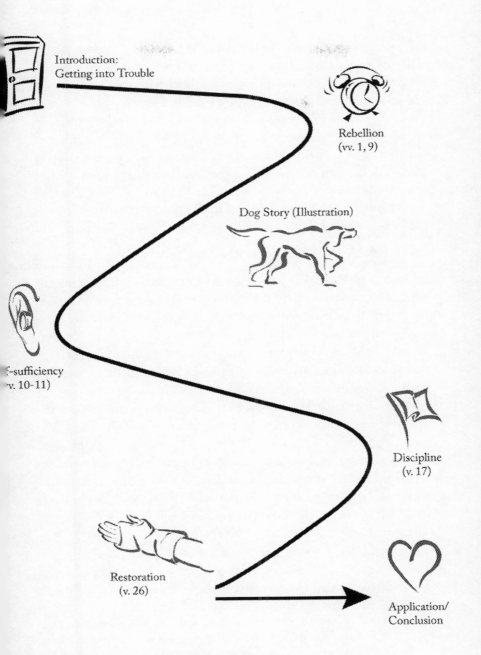

Introduction: Getting into Trouble

Rebellion (vv. 1, 9)

Dog Story (Illustration)

Self-sufficiency (v. 10–11)

Discipline (v. 17)

Restoration (v. 26)

Application/ Conclusion

Sample Road Map for Isaiah 30

by placing four pictures on the page. Sometimes I'll add a couple
other drawings that remind me of extra little stops along the way.
So I might have four major moves, each with an icon or keyword,
and maybe two or three other supplemental or transitional moves
I'll put on the map. Each thing on the map leads to the next thing
sequentially. It has narrative structure and a visual progression.

When I'm done roadmapping, I'm mostly done with my
preparation. With the map I can see the whole thing on one sheet
and could probably put it on a single index card.[13] I can take that
with me up to preach if I want. Or, if I do the next stage of oral
preparation well, I might find I don't even need it by Sunday.

Getting Comfortable with the "Story"

Once the "whole" has been visualized, the road map set, Quintilian recommends a stage of preparation called premeditation. At
this stage, we begin to repeatedly rehearse the terrain of the message until the mental unfolding is natural and unforced: "Indeed,
in general, ideas are more firmly fixed in the memory if our attention does not relax its hold on them by trusting too securely to
writing" (*Institutio oratoria* 10.6.2).

How does premeditation work? It's just running my mind down
a course like water down a streambed. After a while ideas flow
into ideas. Here's Quintilian in his quirky precision: "A habit of
thinking must then be gradually gained by embracing in our minds
a few particulars at first, in such a way that they may be faithfully
repeated. Next, by additions so moderate that our task may scarcely
feel itself increased, our power of conception must be enlarged and
sustained by plenty of exercise" (10.6.3).

Premeditation, since it is done mentally and internally, has
infinite flexibility. Requiring neither light, nor pen and paper, nor
batteries, nor sitting in one place, it allows us to prepare to preach

---

13   In terms of a visual tool for this, visit Prezi at www.prezi.com. Prezi
     presentations are visual roadmaps that put the forest and the trees on one
     page. When I refer to roadmapping, I'm thinking of something that only
     the preacher has in mind. But Prezi brings up other creative options for
     projection of the roadmap for the whole room.

in some fairly weird settings (think walking on the beach, riding a train, laying in bed at night, in the shower, and of course, driving). Premeditation trains the mind in fluency by mentally cementing the sequence of the speech and the connections between sequential points.

But premeditation, though sustained by memory, should not be confused with memorization. Memorization, says Quintilian, will only produce stress since the mind will be engaged on recollection and not on the necessary skill of looking forward, down the mental "road."[14] When premeditation crosses over into memorization, something is lost that cannot be recovered. So instead of writing out the premeditated speech, Quintilian advocates moving not from mind to paper, but from mind to mouth.

As preachers, we can add to this kind of meditation, meditation with God. As we work through the mental progression, it can also be a spiritual exercise where we ask God's help to both understand and explain. When we get to the point of *Rebellion* on our road map, we can pause to admit our own stubbornness before God. We feel it and own it and thank God for his grace to cover it. In this sense, even the stage of premeditating the sermon has more than the sermon in mind. As we sweat to make a good sermon, the sermon also makes us good.

Getting Comfortable with How the Words Come Out

Even more than mentally rehearsing your road map, speaking it ahead of time builds greater fluency and uncovers weakness we wouldn't know about if we hadn't actually tried to preach. Quintilian advocates writing. But his advocacy is more linked

---

14   Hear Quintilian's savvy caution about trying to recollect exact words: "Let our premeditation, therefore, be made with such care that fortune, while she is unable to disappoint, may have it in her power to assist us. But it will depend on the strength of our memory, whether what we have embraced in our minds flows forth easily and does not prevent us, while we are anxious and looking back, and relying on no hope but that of recollection, from casting a glance in advance" (*Institutio oratoria* 10.6.6).

to the construction of general verbal competence than it is the production of a specific message.[15] The caution here is that if we spend most of our preparation time in writing, being slower and more deliberate, we cut ourselves off from expressions forged in the energy of the moment, and likewise the comparative tedium of writing will translate into an undesirable tedium of speech. Writing is a great tool to help clarify and build fluency. But writing is not as well equipped to handle the needs of the moment.[16]

Oral practice, what we might call "pre-hearsing" a speech, will allow us to get comfortable with how the words spill out. Each time we go through it, we find them coming a little more smoothly with a little less stumbling. Quintilian is aware that what sounds best to the ear may be different from what looks best on paper.[17] If we're forced to go one way or the other, it is the ear that should decide what we say. The only way the ear can weigh in on that

---

15   Quintilian notes the cooling effect of writing on a speaker's warm ideas: "But the cause of the fluency is evident, for strongly conceived thoughts and images rising fresh in the mind bear us along with uninterrupted rapidity, when they would sometimes, if retarded by the slowness of writing, grow cool and, if put off, would never return" (*Institutio oratoria* 10.7.14).

16   In his nomination of Quintilian as a postmodern, Frank Macke contrasts speaking and writing: "It is not that I am somehow less rational when I speak, or that my writing requires more of my 'IQ.' It is that I inhabit a body when I write that is different from the one with which I speak, and this is precisely because the site, the topos, of my perception and expression produce a fundamentally different calculus of order and relations." Frank J. Macke, "Quintilian's *Institutio Oratoria* and Postmodern Pedagogy," *American Journal of Semiotics* 17, no. 1 (2001): doi: 10.5840/ajs20011719.

17   Things that look good on paper don't necessarily sound good to the ear. In Quintilian's estimation, "[t]he great judge of composition is the ear, which is sensible of what fills it, misses something in whatever is defective, is offended with what is harsh, soothed with what is gentle, startled by what is distorted, approves what is compact, marks what is lame, and dislikes whatever is redundant and superfluous. Hence, while the learned understand the art of composition, the unlearned enjoy pleasure from it" (*Institutio oratoria* 9.4.116).

decision is to begin speaking the message long before Sunday.

How do we actually do this? Simply put, we start speaking our road map. I've never felt ready to start speaking when I start speaking. I always feel like I should do more preparation. I always, 100 percent of the time, feel like I should tweak something more before I start. This is a trick we play on ourselves to forestall the inevitable. Should we actually start preaching, we might find out we don't like how it's coming out. That would be stressful. So we put off exposing ourselves to the truth. We tell ourselves we need to think a little more first and we keep it in the world of silence. You'll never get the advantage of preaching your sermon beforehand unless you start when you don't feel ready.

Stalling on this or putting it off is a denial of reality. Once our road map is in place, our preparation time is almost up and we must admit it. There is only one last revealing step, and it's one we trick ourselves into thinking is not really necessary. Instead of speaking, we tell ourselves we just need a little more time going over the outline. We put off the moment of speech. But there is no more time. We don't go to the pulpit with the sermon we wish we had, but with the sermon we actually have. So we might as well embrace it and see what's there.

This really requires discipline. But once we force ourselves to start preaching, even when it feels extremely rough, we immediately start to gain clarity. Yes, weaknesses are uncovered, but at least we know where we stand. We are facing reality squarely. We force ourselves to proceed just as if there's an audience. This can be done in an office, in a car in a parking lot, or on a log spanning a river. It doesn't matter where. We just need to get it out of our mouths.

Then, once we preach it, we need a little bit of fixing time. We need to fix some things that were revealed as weak or foggy. But we can't do that until we've declared an end to preparation time. If we don't end our preparation time in a disciplined way, it will continue all the way up through Sunday's opening song. We won't, unless we preach multiple services, have time to fix anything. Even if we do preach in more than one service, doesn't the first service deserve our best too? Must they be the guinea pigs on which we try things out?

Is it possible to over-rehearse? Yes, it is. But I doubt most of us have trouble with that. The danger of overexposing ourselves to our own ideas is that some of the original force of discovery is diluted when phrases become too automatic. There's a sense of the extemporaneous that fuels us forward. Anyone who has preached the same sermon more than three times will confirm this. Your best one will probably be number two or three. After that, it's a slow downhill decline in energy. We're shooting for a natural extemporaneous style, nothing with a hint of the robotic.

A Week in the Life of an Oral Preacher

So how would this play out in an actual week? How does sermon preparation look in this model compared to a more traditional approach? Without advocating a precise formula, I can describe my typical week.

On Monday I review the passage. I say "review" because I already read the book before I ever started this series. I read it before when I decided how fast to proceed and which chapters would be covered in which weeks. It was during this planning stage that I did a lot of the historical backgrounding to the book. That study pays dividends through the entire series because I don't have to do that all over again each week.

So on Monday I just review. I look for things that stand out to me and note questions that arise. I try to pay attention to what provokes me emotionally. I let the passage confuse or irritate or humble me. This might take an hour or so. I can read the chapter ten or fifteen times in just an hour. Sometimes I record myself reading it and listen to it repeatedly. My ears hear my mouth reading it and as a result I get twice the exposure that I'd get in silent reading. As I listen, I invite God into the process. This is where the chapter starts to serve as the devotional focus of my week. I pray through it. I start to internalize it. That's all I do on Monday.

On Tuesday I continue the process of reading and reflecting. I bring the ideas of the chapter to any meetings that day. This is not in a forced way. I'm not shoehorning them in, but I keep them in mind. I dialogue with others about the chapter and hear how it's impacting them. In the course of conversation I might find myself naturally applying the theme or themes to other areas of life. In interactions throughout the week, I turn the passage inside out and think about its implications and difficulties. On the way to an appointment, I turn off the radio and spend the driving time thinking about why this truth is so unappreciated or underapplied. At the end of the day, I spend another hour or two researching any new issues that have arisen from this chapter. This is also when I might spend time in the original languages, which can add additional hours.

On Wednesday morning I pray again about the passage on my morning walk and discuss it with my wife before leaving the house. Later that day I'll also bring it up with the worship leader in the context of worship planning. That afternoon I might find myself in an impromptu counseling situation where the passage comes to mind and fits the situation troubling my friend. These three days I've been conversing about the passage, but resisting the urge to craft a sermon. I need to be concerned, so far, with the truth of the passage, not the sermon. I try not to jump ahead to structuring a sermon until the message of text has been internalized. Here's where I continue to personally wrestle with it. I need to identify how this message speaks to my own fear, jealousy, insecurity, or pride. I ponder these issues instead of what will preach well. I ask myself what this passage offers our people. What do I desire for them? What keeps them from owning and living this message? What changes do I long to see?

On Thursday I move more intentionally toward sequencing ideas as I take my morning walk. I don't carry a notepad. I just start to muse over the flow of thought. I take comfort in the idea that the sermon is already there in the text. I don't need to create it, just let it loose. I start by thinking of a way to open up the topic or main theme. This is the brainstorming that will become my introduction. I look for a way to invite the congregation to come along; a way to plant a real question in their heads. Later that day, I'll decide which sections of the chapter I'll read and which I'll summarize or paraphrase. As I move through the author's flow of thought, his units of thought become stops along my developing road map. I think about how to illustrate and apply those thoughts. I start to see and feel how one thought leads into and supports the next. There is a sense of sequence or flow developing. A sermon starts to emerge. But even at this stage, I still need to keep in mind how this impacts me personally. If it doesn't connect to my real issues, my reanimation of the biblical author's sermon will be hypothetical and disconnected. This process of road mapping might take a couple more hours.

Once I've roughed out my road map I start preaching it before I actually feel ready to preach. Since Friday is my day off, this is on Thursday before I go home, or on Saturday. I find I'm better prepared for Sunday if I preach it on Thursday, but you know how some weeks go. As I begin to speak the sermon, I uncover weakness and/or confusion. This gives me a chance to revise and clarify my thinking. I talk all the way through it out loud. This takes about an hour, but it builds fluency and confidence. Sometime before Sunday I take another half hour to preach it again. I might still consult my road map as I speak, but I'm not dependent on it. Since there's only five to seven stops along the way, I can picture the sequence in my head.

Sunday morning I run through the flow of thought while showering. At this point I don't necessarily speak specific words unless it's still very rough. If I've done my work faithfully, I find an urge to speak starts to build. I feel a readiness and desire to tell someone what I've discovered.

How long does all this take? It varies a lot from week to week. Parts of the process can be timed, and parts really can't (how do we count the time we spend early in the morning, while still in bed, praying through a passage?). But if we consider all the hours listed above, it's in the range of six to ten. While that total might seem inadequate by some standards, I've shifted a good chunk of my preparation time from private study to different kinds of conversation and meditation, which are hard to measure. Praying, talking, and musing are oral ways of grounding and internalization.

On Sunday I need to speak from the inside out and that only comes when, all week long, I "eat the scroll."

In the ancient world, preparation is there under the surface of the speech as bones are hidden under flesh.[18] Our preparation is the engine that quietly but powerfully guides the sermon as it unfolds in the moment.[19] In short, Quintilian is arguing for prepared speeches that have the illusion of being spontaneous. Being prepared at this level takes as much effort as any other method and should never be construed as a time-saving measure. An oral style, though extemporaneous and flexible, is not random or haphazard. After pre-hearsing the sermon, our preparation is finished, but our sermon hasn't even begun yet. As an event, the sermon can't really start without a congregation. In the next chapter we'll finish with some of the challenges of delivery to a live audience.

---

18 In this sense Quintilian is a proponent for natural style as opposed to anything that smacks of the theatrical or exaggerated. Elsewhere he says on this point, "It is not even every gesture or motion that is to be adopted from the actor, for though the orator ought to regulate both to a certain degree, yet he will be far from appearing in a theatrical character and will exhibit nothing extravagant either in his looks, or the movements of his hands, or his walk. If there is any art used by speakers in these points, the first object of it should be that it may not appear to be art" (*Institutio oratoria* 1.11.3).

19 Quintilian stresses how the right kind of memory aids naturalness of speech in the moment: "But a good memory gains us credit even for readiness of wit, as we appear not to have brought what we utter from home, but to have conceived it on the instant, an opinion which is of great service both to the speaker and to his cause, for a judge admires more and distrusts less that which he regards as not having been preconcerted to mislead him" (*Institutio oratoria* 11.2.47).

9

GOING OFF SCRIPT

The Internalized Sermon in the Live Room

For the word to exist, then, we must have several elements present at the same time: duration, two people (the speaker and the listener, who are living in the same moment of time), and concentration on the fact that the past is abolished. The speech is basically presence. It is something alive, and is never an object.

Jacques Ellul, *The Humiliation of the Word*

I grew up in a denomination where preaching was almost a competitive sport. I competed with other would-be teen contenders and had advanced toward the culminating event: the national conference. I won the coveted title "Preacher Boy" and was invited to preach before all the conference delegates, an audience of mostly practicing pastors, their spouses, and other denominational illuminati. This was a big deal.

The air was hot, almost stifling, that summer night in 1979. It had all the elements of a stadium event. Convened in the now-demolished Billy Sunday Tabernacle, the bare lightbulbs and sawdust floor hearkened back to revival culture of midcentury Americana; the days when devout lay folk would spend their vacations to gather at Bible conferences and listen to sermons for eight hours a day. I was in that historic venue. Surely revival would break out. All the lights were on me.

My Compulsion to Preach

Coming from a long line of preachers, I guess I had an advantage. My grandfather was a preacher. I grew up hearing him on occasion and hearing also the folklore surrounding his winsome pulpit mannerisms. He had a natural sense of connection with people and a natural fluency in speaking. My father and three of my uncles followed suit, each trying, in their own ways, to follow in his homiletic footsteps.

My brother, eight years my senior, had in his day also competed in the preaching competition but had never advanced this far. Sensing now, perhaps vicariously, the importance of this moment, he phoned me from across the country to offer his congratulations and also an opening joke. I took his joke and played to the crowd. I told them I felt so much like a real preacher I was sure they wouldn't put a time limit on me. And they laughed. Whatta ya know. I could make people laugh.

It's no surprise that I felt the call to preach that night. Overnight I became a denominational rock star. I had never had so much fun. Was I preaching with wrong motives? Sure. But was that also God's calling? I think so. We can never sort out all the confusing mix of reasons why we have ended up as preachers. But I do know if God only allowed the righteous to preach, there would be a lot of empty pulpits this Sunday. It takes boldness and grace for us to face a congregation knowing as much about ourselves as we do. Voices inside tell us we're either too bad to attempt it or too good for the setting we're in. We alternate between shame and cockiness.

Yet God uses us all the same. He doesn't require us to be flawless. But he does ask us to be honest. Not to claim more than we actually have. Not to hog the spotlight, but share it. His grace frees us to be our flawed selves and invite others to that grace. If we forget that, we don't really have any good news to talk about. But that kind of grace can also foster a freedom of expression. A trust that God will help us speak. A belief that even if we're not precise and polished, that if we're experiencing grace firsthand, that somehow our words will be true and compelling.

Last week I took Augustine's challenge and spent more time in prayer for the sermon than I ever have before. Yet on Sunday I didn't feel differently than any other week. But I am convinced I should do this with or without any noticeable outcome. I shouldn't do it to preach better. I should do it because I'm seeking God wholeheartedly. Because I believe knowing him outside of the sermon is even better than having a great sermon. I believe God will help that kind of preacher preach. I believe that kind of preacher will have freedom of expression that no amount of tedious study or rehearsal can emulate.

So we come at last to the issue of an orally generated style of delivery. We've already seen, in Ong's communication scholarship, the spark he articulates so well. The point where a speaker takes a risk and offers something authentic and personal and maybe a bit clumsy. That's what I'm going to challenge you to do. But I'm not alone in this. Someone else wants to nudge you forward in this too. Let's go back to Quintilian once again.

Extemporaneous Delivery via Memory

In an oral style of speaking, all the preparation that goes into the speech is intended to build to the point of what Quintilian calls "extemporaneous" delivery.[1]

Quintilian is very bold on this. If one cannot master extemporaneous speech, one might as well retire from speaking.[2] For him

---

1   For an extended analysis of Quintilian's advocacy of extemporaneous speech, see Chris Holcomb's "'The Crown of All Our Study': Improvisation in Quintilian's *Institutio Oratoria*," *Rhetoric Society Quarterly* 31, no. 3 (2001): 53–72. Holcomb contends that this is the defining and typically overlooked feature in Quintilian's theory as he sought to distinguish his artful spontaneity from the artless variety practiced by the "delatores" (informers working in the service of the emperors) and, more importantly, from the theory of rhetoric implicit in their oratorical practice (ibid., 55).

2   Quintilian sets a high standard for would-be orators and doesn't mind telling them to try something else if they can't stand and deliver: "But the richest fruit of all our study, and the most ample recompense for the extent of our labor, is the faculty of speaking extempore, and he who has not succeeded in acquiring it will do well, in my opinion, to renounce the

it is the standard to which all preachers should aspire. But having come this far we should also know enough not to confuse extemporaneous with spontaneous or unplanned speeches (properly called "impromptu"). Although there are times when no planning is possible,[3] the general rule is that extemporaneous speech only looks spontaneous. Underneath is the grueling work of good oral preparation.

When Quintilian gets to delivery, he combines it with memory and links it in book 11 of his *Institutes* to *kairos* (the right time as suggested by a live event). Indeed it is memory (not memorization) that fuels delivery: "Accordingly, memory is called, not without reason, the treasury of eloquence" (11.2.1). The memory serves as a sort of storehouse or pantry. It can be stocked with goods that can be recalled as necessary in the *kairos* of the moment. Jesus uses this same metaphor: "Therefore every scribe who has become a disciple of the kingdom of heaven is like a head of a household, who brings out of his treasure things new and old" (Matt. 13:52). This process of building the treasury of the memory is lifelong and starts in childhood.[4]

The memory in this sense is not fixed but fluid. It is a place from which to draw things necessary to the situation at hand. Those without such memory are forced to rely solely upon things

---

occupations of the forum and devote his solitary talent of writing to some other employment" (*Institutio oratoria* 10.7.1).

3   Quintilian sees a place for the written word as something that helps one prepare for the unexpected: "By writing, resources are stored up, as it were, in a sacred repository, from where they may be drawn forth for sudden emergencies or as circumstances require" (*Institutio oratoria* 10.3.3).

4   Referring to boys that have been long exposed to good examples, Quintilian summarizes as follows: "They will have at command, moreover, an abundance of the best words, phrases, and figures, not sought for the occasion, but offering themselves spontaneously, as it were, from a store treasured within them. To this is added the power of quoting the happy expressions of any author, which is agreeable in common conversation and useful in pleading, for phrases which are not coined for the sake of the cause in hand have the greater weight and often gain us more applause than if they were our own" (*Institutio oratoria* 2.7.2).

prepared in advance and can miss opportunities of the moment.[5] This is where the manuscripted speech can limit its own rhetorical power. Written notes, though reassuring, are a poor substitute for the properly prepared force of an incisive memory.[6]

The natural unfolding of a sermon demands the preacher to be "all there" in the room, in the *kairos* of the moment. Every recourse to written prompts pulls the speaker out of the actual room and into the world of abstract thought from which he must continually extricate himself to reenter the sermon. The mind is pulled in too many directions.[7] The preacher is distracted, trying to remember every written word rather than relying on the moment itself to suggest the right words drawn from the pantry of preparation.

Instead of being torn between notes and the present moment, the mind should be engaged in the present while also looking ahead to what comes next.[8] Quintilian is laying out here the magic

---

5   Quintilian sees such unimaginative speakers as woefully disabled to handle a case: "For what can such men produce appropriate to particular causes of which the aspect is perpetually varied and new? How can they reply to questions propounded by the opposite party? How can they at once meet objections or interrogate a witness, when, even on topics of the commonest kind, such as are handled in most causes, they are unable to pursue the most ordinary thoughts in any words but those which they have long before prepared?" (*Institutio oratoria* 2.4.27).

6   Though a strong advocate for writing in terms of general fluency, Quintilian reverses that opinion when it comes to composing a speech: "I even think that we should not write at all what we design to deliver from memory, for if we do so, it generally happens that our thoughts fix us to the studied portions of our speech and do not allow us to try the fortune of the moment. Thus the mind hangs in suspense and perplexity between the two, having lost sight of what was written, and yet not being at liberty to imagine anything new" (*Institutio oratoria* 10.7.32).

7   Here Quintilian points out the danger of loving a certain word or phrase we have crafted ahead of time. It can end up being shoehorned into a sermon instead of flowing naturally: "It will be far safer for him, after treasuring up his matter in his mind, to leave himself at liberty to deliver it as he pleases, for a speaker never loses a single word that he has chosen, without regret, and cannot easily put another in its place while he is trying to recollect the very one that he had written" (*Institutio oratoria* 11.2.48).

8   Quintilian describes the process whereby new ideas flash into the mind

of extemporaneous delivery. The speech progresses on a planned route while simultaneously scanning the moment and the pantry/treasury of memory for extra material that might be fitting. This allows the planned course of the speech to adapt to the moment and even contain elements that are unplanned.[9] It is this balance of both preparation and spontaneity that Quintilian upholds as our standard.

Adaptation to *Kairos*

Becoming more oral frees a preacher to responsibly adjust the path (road map) or respond to a moment. Quintilian's use of *apte* (which the Greeks had earlier called *kairos)* is translated to English as "propriety."[10] It's what prompts the right words for the moment. Our mental map has been premeditated. It is all there, stored up, prepared, even "pre-hearsed" out loud.[11] But our particular congregation on that particular morning drives the actual outpouring of words. This suggests a shared ethos between preacher and congre-

---

even while the current thought is still being expressed: "The ability of speaking extempore seems to me to depend on no other faculty of the mind than this, for while we are uttering one thought, we have to consider what we are to say next, and thus, while the mind is constantly looking forward beyond its immediate object, whatever it finds in the meantime it deposits in the keeping, as it were, of the memory, which, receiving it from the conception, transmits it, as an instrument of intercommunication, to the delivery" (*Institutio oratoria* 11.2.3).

9   Holcomb describes what every preacher has felt at one time or another. "Such moments come to the orator as sudden and brilliant flashes of thought (*extemporales colores*), and should they occur, the orator must be willing and ready to seize the opportunity they present, transitioning seamlessly from the text of his prepared oration into an improvisational mode and back again" (Holcomb, "The Crown of All Our Study," 66).

10   Quntilian loves the perfect word for the moment. "It cannot be too earnestly inculcated that no one can speak with aptitude and propriety unless he considers not only what is to the purpose, but also what is becoming" (*Institutio oratoria* 11.1.8)

11   Quintilian advocates pre-hearsing a speech out loud but also cautions against over-rehearsing, which tends to accidentally remove some of the creative angst needed to keep a preacher "in the moment."

gation where we actually craft our sentences "on the fly." It is the actual audience that is pulling those words out; engaging specific people in a specific place who need this message.

Walter Ong is famous for saying that for a writer, the reader is fiction. That is, one cannot write for nobody or anybody. Since the writers are alone, they must imagine a readership before they can decide what to write.[12] The same is true for us with one distinct advantage. We don't need to imagine an audience because there is a real one sitting right there. While we had to imagine our audience during pre-hearsal, that imagined audience dissolves on Sunday into the real thing. It is those faces looking back—pained, bewildered, skeptical, and sympathetic—it is those faces and no others that will call forth the specific words we utter from the reservoir of our preparation. The preacher who can preach to those faces, and who knows the actual people behind them, will convey an authentic sense of rapport that can't be faked. This is the discovery genre we covered in chapter 6.

This kind of "empathetic and participatory" experience is precisely what Walter Ong identifies as one of the psychodynamics of orality.[13] For a congregation unaccustomed to this level of involvement, the change could be at first confusing. Being suddenly part of the sermon instead of its passive audience takes some getting used to for both preacher and people. But there is no greater respect paid to a flock than to address them from within their moment.

When we can actually read the room midsermon, all sorts of possibilities present themselves: adding an illustration without great hazard, skipping a point on the map and moving more quickly toward the conclusion, or tying in some unexpected intrusion (a chair falling over or a thunderstorm outside). With some discretion we can even refer to people personally ("Greg has to do this. He has to watch his words every time he enters the courtroom as an attorney").[14]

---

12   Ong, *Orality and Literacy*, 100.

13   Ibid., 45.

14   Do this only when you know the person well. Not everybody appreciates

In these kinds of occurrences we signal that we're here together and a part of something unrepeatable. This is in stark contrast to the increasingly popular technology of beaming sermons from centralized master preachers to satellite congregations.[15] While the efficiency is obvious, something vital is lost when we make a congregation eavesdrop on a generic sermon simultaneously covering a dozen different venues.

We've all had the experience of preaching when an illustration came to mind that wasn't part of whatever plan we had. It just pops into our head while we're speaking. Do we take that gift and go with it, or stick to the plan? We have only a fraction of a second to decide. Most of the time I take the chance, and most of the time I don't regret it. Is it too strange to think God might be assisting us in that kind of moment? I know I'm at my greatest dependence when I strike out in this way, leaving, for a while, even my trusty road map.

What about Using Notes?

Like using dialogue in preparation, preaching without notes is not a new idea. Many homiletic theorists have argued for less dependence upon notes and manuscripts. Some try to wean themselves completely away from them via memorization. But merely preaching without notes fails to define truly oral preaching. Oral preaching requires changes to the entire homiletic process and a commitment to honor things that are even more important than preaching. Just getting away from notes is not the point.

In fact, getting rid of notes without restructuring the method of preparation only brings more stress and less true ethos to the sermon. The task of memorization siphons off mental energy from the content and the audience to the task of remembering what comes next. Even at best and with tedious hours of work, Quintil-

---

being suddenly pulled into a sermon.

15   Ong contrasts the physically exhausting personal confrontations of the Lincoln-Douglas debates of 1858 with the sterile and concocted, electronically governed debates of today: "The audience is absent, invisible, inaudible" (*Orality and Literacy*, 135).

ian warns how memorization has a tendency to paralyze a speaker. A memorizing preacher can be, at best, only 90 percent "there."

The simpler way to escape from notes is to never build the original dependence. This requires an intentional move back to Ong's style of orality: the world where speaking was a kind of poetry. Ong is even more pessimistic about writing than Quintilian. He found that learning to read and write "disables the oral poet," since "it introduces into his mind the idea of a text as a controlling narrative and thereby interferes with the oral composing processes."[16] To regain our oral competence we have to consciously toss out our addiction to literary prompts. If we never become dependent on notes, there is no pain in withdrawal. Even if we use visual tools such as the story or road map, the oral preacher never "needs" those tools at the beginning of the process. Starting with the end in mind, we use oral composition to map out natural oral patterns. We learn to organize our speaking instead of speaking our organization. That reversal makes a profound difference inasmuch as we start orally and only use visual prompts as organizational tools. Orality, or what Ong calls the "utterance"[17] is more native to us, and the more natural way to organize.

Learning to preach without memorization or literate prompts frees our eyes to make contact with the audience. Eye contact is a powerful element in ethos. Eyes that engage an audience hold an audience. Every time we look down at notes or up at a screen, eye contact is lost and we encourage minds to wander. It also sends the not-so-subtle message that whatever is being said is "outside" us and must be prompted back to our attention. If the point we're talking about is so trivial that we can't recall it, why should the audience care? We all know intuitively that we do not tend to forget things that are most important. Why would we want to repeatedly telegraph the message "This is so vital, so critical for you to grasp, that I cannot remember it myself and must look down here to figure out where I am"?

---

16   Ibid., 59.
17   Ibid., 165.

Moving from manuscripts or notes to large screen projection of an outline scarcely helps our situation. In either case the audience is constantly diverted from the eyes of the preacher. Despite all the bells and whistles of technology, eyes are still the seat of personal communicative force. To distract them with multiple focal points only dilutes the effect. The persuasive power of a fully engaged speaker, properly prepared, mentally agile, and personally committed remains yet unsurpassed by any screen-based presentation. When used, a screen should merely supplement, not replace the force of the preacher. Putting a lot of text up on the screen further separates the preacher from the content and suggests that the sermon lives somewhere external. With its size and central presence, a screen can easily dominate a speaker and minimize personal force.

It wasn't long after my "Preacher Boy" debut, that I received a card in the mail. It was handwritten by a pastor from the other side of the country, an older preacher I'd never met. He took the time to find my address and jot a few words of encouragement. I remember the phrase "Keep on preaching." Things like that make an impression on a young man. God called me when I was young and a little cocky. But I kept on preaching. And as I have, he has been kind enough to keep working on that cockiness. He wants to replace it with humble dependence. Preaching by ear, from the inside out, pushes me toward stronger internal character and internally driven sermons. When it's risky or scary, it opens us up to that kind of help Jesus talked about when the words will be given to us as a gift, and not from our own wit. Keep on preaching like that.

EPILOGUE

Preaching is admittedly risky. Part of it includes a fear of failing or falling short.[1] But it's that exact fear we need, that fuels us toward the battle. If we're not at least a little afraid, there's no energy and no sense of the stakes involved. God has called us to something noble. Truth is on the line and we need to sense the high calling of preaching his Word in the same way a soldier is sober about the battle ahead.

A Word of Encouragement

We might look at the risk and demands of preaching orally and conclude the risks outweigh the rewards. There are safer, more predictable models. For such a person Quintilian offers some encouragement: "We must endeavor to speak with as much ability as we can, but we must speak according to our ability. For improvement, there is need of application, but not of vexation with ourselves" (*Institutio oratoria* 10.3.14–15). Let's be patient with our development as preachers. We don't step up on Sunday as the preachers we wish we were, but as the preachers we actually are.

---

1   Clearly, Quintilian understood such misgivings: "The fear of failure, moreover, and the expectation of praise for what we shall say gives a spur to our exertions, and it may seem strange that though the pen delights in seclusion and shrinks from the presence of a witness, extemporal oratory is excited by a crowd of listeners, as the soldier by the mustering of the standards. For the necessity of speaking expels and urges forth our thoughts, however difficult to be expressed, and the desire to please increases our efforts. So much does everything look to reward that even eloquence, though it has the highest pleasure in the exercise of its own powers, is yet greatly incited by the enjoyment of praise and reputation" (*Institutio oratoria* 10.7.17).

Back Where We Started

We started with a continuum. On one end were the preachers fairly comfortable on their feet. For those of us toward that end of the spectrum, we need to make sure we're deepening as people even more than as preachers. We can be tempted to use our natural giftedness to cover a lack of deep, prayerful connection to God's Word. We can get by on less, and most people won't notice. At least in any way they can put their finger on. God calls us to make the text nothing less than the ground of our deepest personal devotion in a way that leaks into all things and every task and meeting we have this week. Let's determine to speak of nothing we aren't actually trying on for ourselves. Let's stop repeating our same old funny stories that always get a chuckle and instead ask God for something new and fresh. Something you can't help but say and are convinced is crucial. Let's sit with a text for a long time without trying to preach it. Get to the crucial, not the trivial. The real condition of things, not theoretical advice you picked up from others. Let's speak from the heart.

On the other end of the scale is the preacher who doesn't feel gifted with words and struggles with fluency. Those of us here have things we desperately want to say, but we're afraid of how they'll come out. Our temptation is to cover that vulnerability with the precision of writing. Writing is not the enemy. Writing things out ahead of time does clarify and can be a great tool. But at some point, we need to get the ideas moving less off the page and more out of our mouths. More than our precision, people need our hearts. Let's trust our good, deep, and prayerful preparation. Trust God to give us the words. Let's take a risk. Start a sentence and let the faces of the people help to finish it. Let's speak to these people right in front of us and quit worrying about being smooth. Smooth and polished can become an idol that we should turn from. A sincere heart covers a multitude of oratorical sins. Let's speak from that heart.

BIBLIOGRAPHY

Aquinas, Thomas. *The "Summa Theologica" of St. Thomas Aquinas.
Parts II–III* [*Summa Theologica*]. Translated by Fathers of the English
Dominican Province. Vols. 1–2. 1st complete American ed. New
York: Benzinger Bros., 1947.

Aristotle. *Rhetoric* [*Rhetorica*]. In *The Rhetoric and the Poetics of Aristotle.*
Translated by W. Rhys Roberts (1924) and Ingram Bywater
(1909), respectively. Reprinted with an introduction by Edward P. J.
Corbett. New York: Random House, 1954. Reprint, 1984. Originally
published as *Rhetorica*, The Works of Aristotle 11 (Oxford:
Clarendon Press, 1924).

Augustine. *On Christian Doctrine* [*De doctrina christiana*]. Translated by
D. W. Robertson Jr. Upper Saddle River, NJ: Prentice-Hall, 1958.

Augustine. *Treatises (341–400) on Various Subjects.* New York: New City
Press, 1995.

Bakhtin, M. M. *Speech Genres and Other Late Essays.* Edited by Caryl
Emerson and Michael Holquist. Translated by Vern W. McGee.
Austin: University of Texas Press, 1986. First published in Russian in
1979.

Baldwin, Neil. *Edison: Inventing the Century.* Chicago: University of
Chicago Press, 2001. Originally published in 1995 by Hyperion.

Bertonneau, Thomas F. "Orality, Literacy, and the Tradition." *Modern
Age* 45, no. 2 (2003): 113–22.

Bizzell, Patricia, and Bruce Herzberg, eds. *The Rhetorical Tradition:
Readings from Classical Times to the Present.* 2nd ed. Boston: Bedford/
St. Martins, 2001. First published in 1990.

Black, M. H. "The Printed Bible." In *The West from the Reformation to
the Present Day.* Edited by S. L. Greenslade. Vol. 3 of *The Cambridge
History of the Bible.* Cambridge: Cambridge University Press, 1963.

Brandenburg, Earnest. "Quintilian and the Good Orator." *Quarterly
Journal of Speech* 34, no. 1 (1948): 23–39.

Brinton, Alan. "Quintilian, Plato, and the *Vir Bonus.*" *Philosophy and
Rhetoric* 16, no. 3 (1983): 167–86.

Buber, Martin. *Between Man and Man*. London: Routledge Classics, 2002.

Burton-Christie, Douglas. "Listening, Reading, and Praying: Orality,
    Literacy and Early Monastic Spirituality." *Anglican Theological
    Review* 83, no. 2 (2001): 197–221.

Buttrick, David. *Homiletic: Moves and Structures*. Philadelphia: Fortress,
    1987.

Calvin, John. *Institutes of the Christian Religion*. Translated by Ford Lewis
    Battles. Edited by John T. McNeill. 2 vols. Library of Christian
    Classics 20–21. Philadelphia: Westminster, 1960.

Clarkson, Thomas. "A Portraiture of Quakerism." *Friends Intelligencer* 13
    (1866): 17–18.

Colson, F. H. "Quintilian, the Gospels and Christianity." *Classical
    Review* 39, nos. 7–8 (1925): 166–70.

Davis, Jeffry C. "The Virtue of Liberal Arts: Quintilian and Character
    Education." *Journal of Interdisciplinary Studies* 19, nos. 1/2 (2007):
    61–80.

Edwards, James R. *The Gospel according to Mark*. Grand Rapids:
    Eerdmans, 2002.

Ellul, Jacques. *The Humiliation of the Word*. Grand Rapids: Eerdmans, 1985.

Enos, Richard Leo. *Roman Rhetoric: Revolution and the Greek Influence*.
    Prospect Heights, IL: Waveland, 1995.

Fant, Clyde. *Preaching for Today*. New York: Harper & Row, 1975.

Greenslade, S. L. "Epilogue." In *The West from the Reformation to the
    Present Day*. Edited by S. L. Greenslade. Vol. 3 of *The Cambridge
    History of the Bible*. Cambridge: Cambridge University Press, 1963.

Harris, James Henry. *The Word Made Plain: The Power and Promise of
    Preaching*. Minneapolis: Augsburg, 2004.

Harris, William V. *Ancient Literacy*. Cambridge: Harvard University Press,
    1989.

Havelock, Eric A. *The Muse Learns to Write: Reflections on Orality
    and Literacy from Antiquity to the Present*. New Haven, CT: Yale
    University Press, 1988.

Holcomb, Chris. "'The Crown of All Our Study': Improvisation in
    Quintilian's *Institutio Oratoria*." *Rhetoric Society Quarterly* 31, no. 3
    (2001): 53–72.

Hong, Howard V. and Edna H. Hong, ed. and trans. *Søren Kierkegaard's
    Journals and Papers*. Vol. 3. Bloomfield: Indiana University Press, 1975.

Horsley, Richard A. *Performing the Gospel: Orality, Memory and Mark.* Minneapolis: Fortress, 2006.

Kierkegaard, Søren. *Papers and Journals: A Selection.* Translated by Alastair Hannay. New York: Penguin Books, 1996.

Kuyper, Abraham. *Common Grace.* Translated by Nelson D. Kloosterman and Ed M. van der Maas. Edited by Jordan J. Ballor and Stephen J. Grabill. 3 vols. Grand Rapids: CLP Academic, 2013–.

LaRue, Cleophus J. *The Heart of Black Preaching.* Louisville: Westminster John Knox, 2000.

———. *Power in the Pulpit: How America's Most Effective Black Preachers Prepare Their Sermons.* Louisville: Westminster John Knox, 2002.

Logie, John. "'I Have No Predecessor to Guide My Steps': Quintilian and Roman Authorship." *Rhetoric Review* 22, no. 4 (2003): 353–73.

Lowry, Eugene L. *The Homiletical Plot: The Sermon as Narrative Art Form.* Rev. ed. Louisville: Westminster John Knox, 2001. First published in 1980.

Macke, Frank J. "Quintilian's *Institutio Oratoria* and Postmodern Pedagogy." *American Journal of Semiotics* 17, no. 1 (2001): 183–202. doi: 10.5840/ajs20011719.

McLuhan, Marshall. *The Gutenberg Galaxy: The Making of Typograhic Man.* Toronto: University of Toronto Press, 1962.

Mendelson, Michael. "Quintilian and the Pedagogy of Argument." *Argumentation* 15 no. 3 (2001): 277–94.

Mitchell, Henry H. *Black Preaching: The Recovery of a Powerful Art.* Nashville: Abingdon, 1990.

———. *Celebration and Experience in Preaching.* Rev. ed. Nashville: Abingdon, 2010. First published, 1990.

Murphy, J. J. "Saint Augustine and the Debate about a Christian Rhetoric." *Quarterly Journal of Speech* 46, no. 4 (1960): 400–410.

Niditch, Susan. *Oral World and Written Word: Ancient Israelite Literature.* Louisville: Westminster John Knox, 1996.

Ong, Walter J. *Interfaces of the Word: Studies in the Evolution of Consciousness and Culture.* Ithaca, NY: Cornell University Press, 1977.

———. "Literacy and Orality in Our Times." *Journal of Communication* 30, no. 1 (1980): 197–204.

———. *An Ong Reader: Challenges for Further Inquiry.* Edited by Thomas J. Farrell and Paul A. Soukoup. Cresskill, NJ: Hampton, 2002.

————. "Oral Residue in Tudor Prose Style." *PMLA* 80, no. 3 (1965): 145–54. *PMLA* is the journal of the Modern Language Association of America.

————. *Orality and Literacy: The Technologizing of the Word.* 2nd ed. New York: Routledge, 2002. First published in 1982 by Methuen & Co. Ltd. Page citations are to the Routledge edition.

————. *The Presence of the Word: Some Prolegomena for Cultural and Religious History.* New Haven, CT: Yale University Press, 1967.

————. Review of *Arguments in Rhetoric against Quintilian: Translation and Text of Peter Ramus's* Rhetoricae Distinctiones in Quintilianum *(1549),* by Peter Ramus, translation by Carole Newlands. *Quarterly Journal of Speech* 72, no. 2 (1987): 242–43.

————. "Voice as Summons for Belief: Literature, Faith, and the Divided Self." *Thought* 33, no. 1 (1958): 43–61.

Pagitt, Doug. *Preaching Re-Imagined.* Grand Rapids: Zondervan, 2005.

Pasquarello, Michael, III. *Sacred Rhetoric: Preaching as a Theological and Pastoral Practice of the Church.* Grand Rapids: Eerdmans, 2005.

Plato. *Phaedrus.* In *Euthyphro. Apology. Crito. Phaedo. Phaedrus.* Vol. 1 of *Plato: In Twelve Volumes.* Translated by Harold North Fowler. Loeb Classical Library 36. Cambridge: Harvard University Press, 1914. Reprint, 2005.

————. *Gorgias.* New York: Classic Books America, 2009.

Polkinghorne, John. *Exploring Reality: The Intertwining of Science and Theology.* New Haven, CT: Yale University Press, 2006.

Quintilian. *Institutes of Oratory* [*Institutio oratoria*]. Edited by Lee Honeycutt. Translated by John Selby Watson. Hypertextual reprint edition of the 1856 Watson translation. Ames: Iowa State University, 2006. Originally published as *Quintilian's Institutes of Oratory; or The Education of an Orator,* trans. John Selby Watson (London: Henry G. Bohn, 1856). http://rhetoric.eserver.org/quintilian/.

Reed, Walter L. *Dialogues of the Word: The Bible as Literature according to Bakhtin.* Oxford: Oxford University Press, 1993.

Richards, E. Randolph. *The Secretary in the Letters of Paul.* WUNT II 42. Tübingen: J. C. B Mohr (Paul Siebeck), 1991. Based on Randolph's PhD dissertation published in 1988.

Schaeffer, John D. "The Dialectic of Orality and Literacy: The Case of Book 4 of Augustine's *De doctrina christiana,*" *PMLA* 111, no. 5 (1996): 1133–44.

Schökel, Luis Alonso. *The Inspired Word: Scripture in the Light of Language and Literature.* Translated by Francis Martin. New York: Herder and Herder, 1965.

Shields, Bruce E. *From the Housetops: Preaching in the Early Church and Today.* St. Louis: Chalice Press, 2000.

Soukoup, Paul A. "Contexts of Faith: The Religious Foundation of Walter Ong's Literacy and Orality." *Journal of Media and Religion* 5, no. 3 (2006): 175–88.

Sullivan, Dale L. "The Ethos of Epideictic Encounter." *Philosophy and Rhetoric* 26, no. 2 (1993): 113–33.

Webb, Stephen. *The Divine Voice: The Christian Proclamation and the Theology of Sound.* Grand Rapids: Brazos, 2004.

Wilken, Robert Louis. *The Spirit of Early Christian Thought: Seeking the Face of God.* New Haven, CT: Yale University Press, 2003.

SCRIPTURE INDEX

GENERAL INDEX

Dave McClellan is pastor of The Chapel at Tinkers Creek in Streetsboro, Ohio, and adjunct professor at Indiana Wesleyan University, Trinity Evangelical Divinity School, and John Carroll University. He received a Bachelor of Science in Communication from Grace College and a Master of Divinity from Denver Seminary before completing a Doctor of Philosophy in Rhetoric and Communication from Duquesne University. Dave has served as an editor for *Homiletics* and contributed to the *Journal of the Evangelical Homiletic Society*, *Leadership Journal*, and *Preaching Today*. He's married to Karen, and they have two grown children.

Printed in the United States
by Baker & Taylor Publisher Services